The Illustrated
Afghan

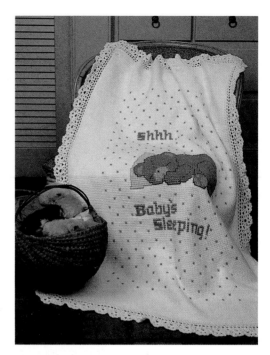

The Illustrated Afghan

by Leslie Linsley

Photographs by Jon Aron

Sedgewood® Press
New York

For Sedgewood® Press:

Director: *Elizabeth P. Rice*
Project Manager: *Barbara Machtiger*
Project Editor: *Patricia Bevans*
Production Manager: *Bill Rose*
Cover & Graphic Design: *Diane Wagner*
Photos pages 32–33, 60–61, 126–127: *Robert Gattullo*

Illustrations: *Robby Smith*
Additional Photographs: *"Country Tulips" courtesy Susan Bates, Inc.*
"Shh, Baby Sleeping" and "Hearts and
Flowers" courtesy Bernat Yarn and Craft Co.
"Bouquet of Roses," cover photograph by
David Frazier, courtesy Family Circle *magazine*

Dear Crafter:
We thank you for choosing *The Illustrated Afghan* and are sure you'll enjoy making projects from the many beautiful selections in the book.

Here is a chance to combine two favorite needlecrafts—crochet and cross-stitch—to make one glorious afghan. After crocheting the background "canvas," you cross-stitch the design on the grid formed by the afghan stitches. Choose from an array of country, floral, and nursery designs. Then follow Leslie Linsley's clear, detailed instructions and cross-stitch charts to make pretty-as-a-picture afghans to treasure in your own home setting or to give as gifts.

We at Sedgewood Press are very proud of the craft books we publish. They are of the highest quality and offer projects for every level of crafting skill. Our books feature large, full-color photographs of all projects, instructions and charts that are simple and readable, and projects that encompass a range of designs and uses.

We hope you'll use *The Illustrated Afghan* with pleasure and that you'll be as proud of your creation as we are of ours.

Barbara S. Machtiger
Editorial Project Manager
Sedgewood® Press

Acknowledgments

I would like to thank all the experienced needleartists listed below who spent hours making the afghans for this book, and especially my mother, Ruth Linsley, who always says "yes" when I ask for her help.

Needleworkers
Margaret Hendrickson
Sylvia Kaplan
Else Knudsen
Ruth Linsley
Robin Murray
Corinne Nicholas
Ines Pleschutzinig
Joan Roche
Mary Smith
Marion Tuthill

I would like to extend my appreciation to the yarn manufacturers and distributors who have lent their support and have been most helpful in the preparation of this book. They are:
Bernat Yarn and Craft Co., Uxbridge, MA
Brunswick Yarn Co., Pickens, SC
Coats & Clark, Jacksonville, FL
DMC, Elizabeth, NJ
Johnson Creative Arts, West Townsend, MA
Susan Bates, Inc., Chester, CT
Tahki Imports, Ltd., Moonachie, NJ
Wm Unger & Co., Bridgeport, CT

And finally I'd like to thank my friends and neighbors in Nantucket who graciously allowed us into their homes and gardens to photograph the afghans, especially Rene and Norman Beach and Ginny and Joe Beaulieu.

Contents

Introduction

Last year Jon and I designed a feature story on decorating with a blue and white theme for *Family Circle* magazine. For the bedroom we chose a rose chintz fabric, a design that has become quite popular. We made a quilt for the bed and had a slipper chair covered with matching fabric. We decided that what the room needed was the softening effect of a pretty lap throw that could be made easily. Since both crocheting and cross-stitch are such popular crafts, we designed a lap blanket using the afghan stitch over which we created a bouquet of roses in cross-stitching. It was an immediate success and led to the idea for this book.

Later that year I traveled to Chicago to accept the T.E.N. award which was a great honor bestowed on me by the National Needlework Association. T.E.N. stands for "tribute to excellence in needlework" and the award was given to me for promoting the needlearts in this country. It was an exciting event attended by over 1,200 representatives of the needleart retailers from every state as well as editors from all the magazines. The best time for me was having the opportunity to talk to store owners and buyers who are helping craftworkers with their projects and getting feedback on what they most enjoy doing in their spare time. And it was a chance to ask as many as possible what they thought about a book filled with afghans illustrated with cross-stitching. The enthusiastic response made me anxious to get back to the Nantucket studio to relate my findings to Jon so we could get busy designing afghans.

Next, I called a few of the manufacturers whose yarn I often use to ask what they thought of the idea. Eleanor Bernat, president of Bernat Yarn and Craft Company, was most supportive. She told me that whenever they present such an afghan it is well received and becomes a treasured object by those who make it. At the Wm. Unger Company I spoke with President Bob Lilley, who also told me of their success with two illustrated afghans. Both companies generously offered to share their designs with us.

Many of the women on Nantucket, where I live part of the year, are talented crocheters and also enjoy doing cross-stitch. Their work on the afghans was most helpful in assuring that we could finish the book within a reasonable time frame. For months Jon and I cross-stitched the designs and now that the book is finished I miss having my cross-stitch projects to work on. What I discovered from making so many projects, one right after the other, is that cross-stitching over yarn is quick and easy, unlike cross-stitching on even-weave Aida cloth. Watching a large picture emerge over the soft "canvas" background is a rewarding experience you'll enjoy no matter which design you choose.

For the most part, the afghans are quick and easy to make. The panels on which the design is worked are made of the afghan stitch. Once you get into the rhythm, the work goes automatically. A friend of my daughter Robby's is an exchange student from Norway. Elsa knew how to crochet but had never done the afghan stitch. It took a while to teach her, since she had never read crochet directions in English before. But once she got going it was a cinch. Every time we saw her she had a crochet hook and yarn in her hand. And when she showed up at the studio without her yarn work we wanted to know why. She even took her squares for the clown afghan on page 154 with her on vacation to Florida.

On Nantucket Island we have town meetings as a form of local government. They often go on for hours. When I look around the auditorium at the hundreds of people gathered there, every other person has a yarn project in her lap. I must admit, it's hard to find a man with a crochet hook in his hand, but the women use the time to make headway on their afghans. Jon refuses to go out in public with his cross-stitching, but in truth he's much better at it than I am and is most critical when I make an error and tell him to photograph the project so my errors don't show. Ultimately he shames me into ripping them out and starting over.

Crochet is a craft that many people enjoy doing. So we felt that adding another craft that is equally enjoyable would be even more appealing. Sometimes a crocheted afghan has been passed down in a family and has special meaning to those who use it. Perhaps a grandmother has made a crocheted christening blanket for a new baby. Often a college-bound student will take a lovingly made afghan off to school with him or her. These items become family heirlooms, passed from one generation to another. I still have an old granny-square afghan that my grandmother made for my mother. It's a bit worn out but I love it for sentimental reasons. The illustrated designs on the afghans presented here make them all the more personal.

Many young women are expressing an interest in learning to crochet. They want to make things for their homes. Crocheting can often be more satisfying than other crafts. And in the end, the projects are practical, inexpensive, and good-looking. Crochet is a versatile craft. You can make an afghan for any season, depending on the yarn you choose.

While most of the projects in this book are quick and easy, they are not intended only for beginners. There are many projects with challenging stitches and there are certainly no compromises in regard to design. I hope you'll enjoy making them as much as we did.

The Basics

Crochet Basics

All of the afghans in this book use the basic afghan stitch to create the background "canvas" for the cross-stitch illustrations. The borders, granny squares, panels, etc., that complete some of the afghans are made with a few basic crochet stitches.

The work starts with a chain made up of a series of loops on a crochet hook. Unlike knitting, which is done on two, three, and sometimes four needles, crocheting is done on a single hook. Hooks come in various sizes. The size you use will depend on the yarn, pattern, and project. Sometimes a project calls for an afghan hook as well as a crochet hook. An afghan hook is longer than a crochet hook, with a flat-headed end like a knitting needle so the stitches won't fall off. It is used for the afghan stitch when creating a large material.

Most of the yarns used for the afghans shown here are knitting worsted or sport weight and they are washable. However, after putting so much time and effort into creating the project, you may want to have the afghan dry-cleaned when it is necessary to do so.

CHAIN STITCH (ch)

The beginning of every project in crochet is a row of a specific number of chain stitches. These are the basis of the piece, just as the cast-on row is the basis of a knit piece.

At the beginning of every row, an extra chain stitch (or stitches, in the case of double and treble crochet) is made. This is counted as the first stitch of the next row and is called the turning chain. In these instructions, each chain stitch is simply called a chain (ch). When a string of chain stitches is being discussed, it is known by the number of stitches, for example, "first ch-5" means the first group of chain stitches in a row.)

1. Make a slip knot by taking yarn about 2 inches from the end and winding it once around your middle three fingers.

2. Draw a length of yarn through the loop around your fingers. Put this new loop on your crochet hook and pull tight.

3. With yarn wound over left-hand fingers, pass the hook under the yarn on index finger and catch a strand with the hook (Figure 1).

4. Draw the yarn through the loop already on the hook to make 1 chain stitch (ch) (Figure 2).

Repeat steps 3 and 4 for as many chain stitches as needed. If you hold the chain as close to the hook as possible with the thumb and index finger of your left hand, the chain will be even.

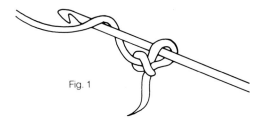

Fig. 1

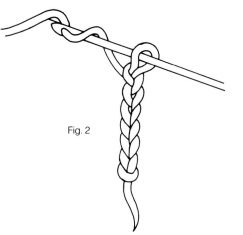

Fig. 2

SINGLE CROCHET (sc)

1. After making the initial chain, insert the hook in the 2nd chain from the hook (the skipped chain is the turning chain) and bring the yarn over the hook from the back to the front (clockwise) (Figure 1). Draw the yarn through the chain so you have 2 loops on the hook, as shown in Figure 2.

2. Bring the yarn over the hook again and draw the hook with its 3rd loop through the 2 loops already on the hook. You have made 1 single crochet (sc).

3. Repeat steps 1 and 2 into each chain stitch across the row (Figure 3). At the end of the row, make 1 chain (ch 1) and turn the work around from right to left so the reverse side is facing you.

4. The turning chain stitch counts as the first stitch of the next row. Work the next single crochet by inserting the hook under the 2 top loops of the next stitch in the previous row. Continue by working a single crochet in each stitch across the row. Work a single crochet in the ch-1 (turning chain). Chain 1 and turn.

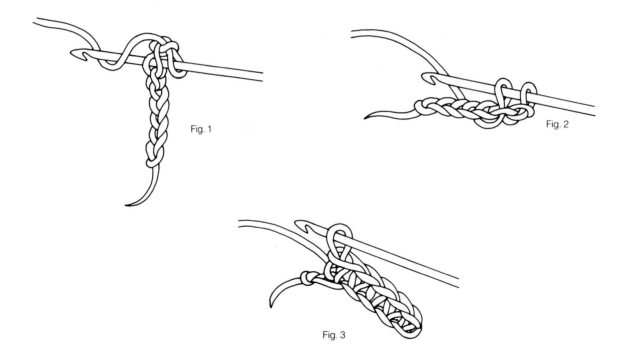

Fig. 1

Fig. 2

Fig. 3

14

FASTENING OFF

At the end of all required rows or rounds, cut the yarn with a tail of 2 or 3 inches and draw it through the last loop at the end of the row. Pull tight and weave it into the fabric with a yarn needle. Sometimes the tail is used to sew pieces together. If this is the case, leave a tail that is long enough. Sometimes directions will say ''break off,'' which is the same as fasten off.

DOUBLE CROCHET (dc)

1. After making the initial chain, bring the yarn over the hook and insert the hook, from front to back, into the 4th chain from the hook (the skipped chains are the turning chains) (Figure 1).
2. Yarn over hook. Draw through chain. There are now 3 loops on the hook (Figure 2).
3. Yarn over hook. Draw through 2 loops on the hook. There are now 2 loops on the hook (Figure 3).
4. Yarn over hook. Draw the yarn through the last 2 loops on the hook (Figure 4). One double crochet (dc) is completed.

Yarn over hook, insert hook into next chain stitch, and repeat steps 2, 3, and 4.

Repeat into each chain stitch across the row. At the end of the row, make 3 chains (ch-3) and turn the work around from right to left so the reverse side is facing you.

The turning chain counts as the first stitch of the next row. Work the next double crochet by bringing the yarn over the hook and inserting the hook under the 2 top loops of the next stitch in the previous row. Continue by working a double crochet in each stitch across the row. Work a double crochet in the 3rd stitch of the ch-3 (turning chain). Chain 3 and turn.

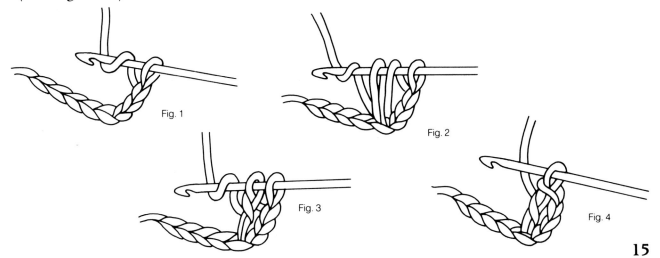

Fig. 1

Fig. 2

Fig. 3

Fig. 4

15

HALF DOUBLE CROCHET (hdc)

1. After making the initial chain, bring the yarn over the hook and insert the hook, from front to back, into the 3rd chain from the hook (the skipped chains are the turning chains) (Figure 1).

2. Yarn over hook. Draw through chain. There are now 3 loops on the hook (Figure 2).

3. Yarn over hook (Figure 3). Draw through all 3 loops. One half double crochet (hdc) is completed (Figure 4). Yarn over hook, insert hook into next chain stitch, and repeat steps 2 and 3.

Repeat into each chain stitch across the row. At the end of the row, make 2 chains (ch 2) and turn the work around from right to left so the reverse side is facing you.

The turning chain counts as the first stitch of the next row. Work the next half double crochet by bringing the yarn over the hook and inserting the hook under the 2 top loops of the next stitch of the previous row. Continue by working a half double crochet in each stitch across the row. Work a half double crochet in the ch-2 turning chain. Chain 2 and turn.

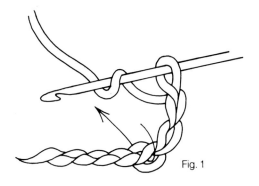

Fig. 1

Fig. 2

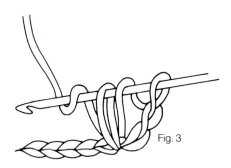

Fig. 3

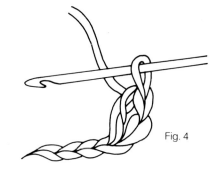

Fig. 4

16

TREBLE OR TRIPLE CROCHET (tr)

1. After making the initial chain, wind the yarn around the hook twice (Figure 1) and insert the hook, from front to back, into the 5th chain from the hook (the skipped chains are the turning chains).
2. Yarn over hook. Draw through chain. There are now 4 loops on the hook.
3. Yarn over hook. Draw through 2 loops (Figure 2). There are now 3 loops on the hook.
4. Yarn over hook. Draw through 2 loops (Figure 3). There are now 2 loops on the hook.
5. Yarn over hook. Draw through the last 2 loops (Figure 4). One triple crochet (tr) is completed. Wind the yarn around the hook twice, insert the hook into the next chain stitch, and repeat steps, 2, 3, 4, and 5.

Repeat into each chain stitch across the row. At the end of the row, make 4 chains (ch 4) and turn the work around from right to left so the reverse side is facing you.

The turning chains count as the first stitch of the next row. Work the next triple crochet by winding the yarn around the hook twice and inserting the hook under the 2 top loops of the next stitch in the previous row. Continue by working a triple crochet in each stitch across the row. Work a triple crochet in the ch-4 turning chain. Chain 4 and turn.

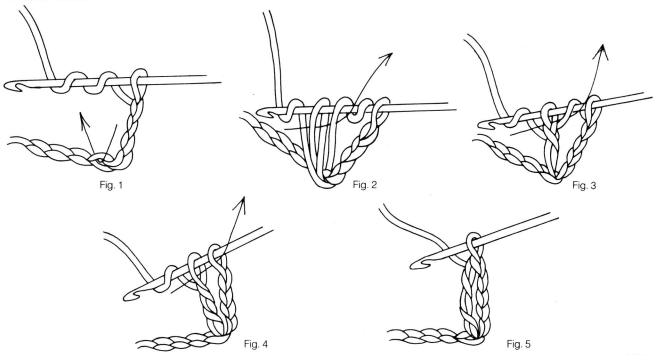

Fig. 1   Fig. 2   Fig. 3

Fig. 4   Fig. 5

DOUBLE TREBLE OR TRIPLE CROCHET (dtr)

1. After making the initial chain, wind the yarn around the hook 3 times and insert the hook, from front to back, into the 6th chain from the hook (the skipped chains are the turning chains).
2. Yarn over hook. Draw through the chain. There are now 5 loops on the hook.
3. Yarn over hook. Draw through 2 loops. There are now 4 loops on the chain.
4. Repeat 3 more times until there is one loop left on the hook. One double triple crochet (dtr) is completed.

TURNING

You will need a number of chain stitches at the end of each row to bring your work into position for the next row. The number of chain stitches depends on the crochet stitch you are working. For single crochet you will ch 1 to turn; for half double crochet, you will ch 2; for double crochet, you will ch 3; and for treble or triple crochet you will ch 4.

SLIP STITCH (sl st)

Insert the hook into the chain (Figure 1). Yarn over hook. Draw through both the chain and the loop on the hook in one motion (Figure 2). One slip stitch (sl) is completed. A slip stitch is used to join a chain in order to form a ring. Insert the hook under the top strand of the stitch. Yarn over the hook. Draw through both the stitch and the loop on the hook in one motion.

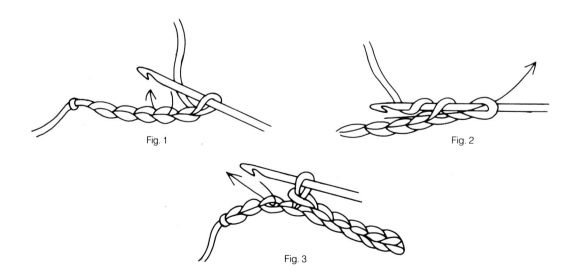

Fig. 1

Fig. 2

Fig. 3

18

WORKING IN SPACES

In crochet work that is lacy and contains openwork, often a stitch in the preceding row is skipped and you will be instructed to chain across the gap. Sometimes the pattern tells you to work stitches in a space instead of in a stitch. In that case, insert your hook through the gap or space (sp) rather than through a stitch in the preceding row. Often several stitches are worked in 1 space, as a way of increasing stitches.

INCREASING SINGLE CROCHET (inc)

When a pattern calls for an increase of a single crochet, work 2 stitches in 1 stitch (Figure 1).

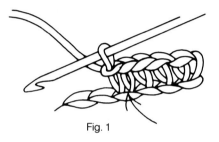

Fig. 1

DECREASING SINGLE CROCHET (dec)

When a pattern calls for a decrease of a single crochet, draw up a loop in 1 stitch, then draw up a loop in the next stitch so there are 3 loops on your hook (Figure 1). Yarn over hook and draw through all 3 loops at once (Figure 2).

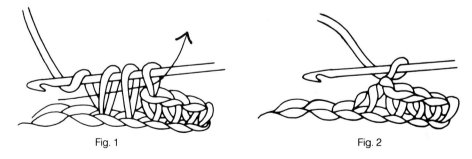

Fig. 1   Fig. 2

WORKING EVEN

This means to continue in the same manner without either increasing or decreasing stitches.

19

AFGHAN STITCH

Almost all the projects in this book employ the afghan stitch. This is the stitch most commonly used to create a background material over which you will work your cross-stitch design. The afghan stitch produces even rows of square boxes much like an even-weave fabric such as linen or Aida cloth. Refer to the following directions before beginning one of the afghan projects.

Row 1: Draw up a loop in each stitch of initial chain, leaving all loops on hook as shown in Figure 1. Take loops off as follows: Yarn over (yo) hook, draw through 1 loop, *yo hook, draw through 2 loops, repeat from * across the row as shown in Figure 2. The loop remaining on the hook counts as the first loop of the next row (Figure 3).

Row 2: Skip the first upright bar. Insert the hook from right to left under the next upright bar. Yarn over and draw up a loop. Repeat into each remaining upright bar, leaving all loops on the hook. Take loops off in the same way as Row 1. Repeat only Row 2 for desired length (Figure 4).

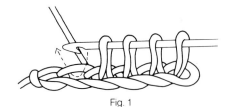

Fig. 1

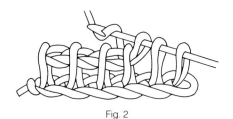

Fig. 2

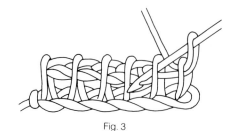

Fig. 3

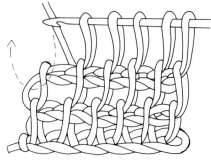

Fig. 4

CROSS-STITCH OVER AFGHAN STITCH

Each upright bar across the row of afghan stitch is counted as 1 stitch. When a cross-stitch design is indicated for a project, you will be provided with a chart. Follow the chart and count upright bars. There are 2 holes formed by the afghan stitch *after* each upright bar.

Working from left to right, join color on wrong side at the lower hole and work across the next upright bar to the upper hole. Then bring the needle through the lower hole directly below as shown in Figure 5. Continue for the number of stitches in the color being used. Then work from right to left to form a cross. Do not pull yarn too tight.

Crocheting Tips

YARN

There are many different yarns available for crochet. Yarns are grouped according to weight, meaning their thickness. The basic types of yarn are bulky weight, worsted weight, sport weight, and baby weight. The bulky yarn is the thickest and baby weight the thinnest. Most crochet projects, especially afghans, are made with worsted weight, which is the most popular because it's the easiest to work with.

Yarns are made of different materials. Most are made either of natural fibers such as wool, cotton, linen, or mohair or of synthetic fibers such as acrylic, nylon, orlon, and rayon. Many yarns are blends of several types of fibers. When you buy yarn the label will give you all this information.

Hints about buying yarn: Be sure to select yarn of the weight recommended in the project directions. Buy enough yarn to complete the project because it is often difficult to match colors exactly. Each time yarn is dyed it varies slightly. Check the dye lot number on the skeins to be sure that all the yarn you buy is from the same dye lot.

CROCHET HOOKS AND NEEDLES

Hooks come in many different sizes. Generally, the thicker the yarn, the thicker the hook you will use. The size of the hook and the thickness of the yarn determines the size of the stitches. If you change the type of yarn or size hook recommended with each project, the finished afghan will not work out to be the size indicated.

A large blunt sewing needle with a large eye is called a tapestry or yarn needle. This is used for sewing finished project pieces together and for weaving in yarn ends. This needle is also used for the cross-stitching. I prefer the plastic needles, but they are also made of steel and aluminum.

GAUGE

Every needleworker crochets a little bit differently. Some hold the yarn tightly, others loosely, some pull the hook through a little further, some not quite so far. Because of individual differences, two people can work with the same materials, yet end up with finished pieces of different sizes.

Since people work differently, crochet patterns cannot just state the size hook and weight of yarn you should use. Crochet instructions state the number of stitches to the inch that you must get for your project to come out the right size. The required number of stitches to the inch is called the gauge. Sometimes the pattern will also give you a row gauge, meaning the number of rows to the inch, which I've done with the afghan patterns in this book.

When you are doing cross-stitch over the afghan stitch you are working from a chart of squares that correspond to the number of squares on your afghan. The size of your finished piece is extremely important to the success of your finished project. It's essential to get the correct gauge.

Each project will suggest the type of yarn you should use and the hook size. But how you crochet, in regard to tension, etc., as described above, will determine the proper gauge. For this reason, I suggest that you start by making a test square of approximately 4 × 4 inches, using the yarn, hook, and stitch pattern recommended. This will give you a chance to see the yarn made up as well as to check the gauge before beginning the project. Count the number of stitches that should equal the given inches and mark with pins at the beginning and end. With a tape measure on the flat swatch, check to see if they correspond. If you have fewer stitches per inch than the pattern calls for, your work is too loose. Change to a smaller hook. If you have more stitches per inch than you should, go up one hook size. Make another swatch to be sure the gauge is correct, and adjust accordingly. Check the gauge for rows as well as for stitches.

MOTIF

A motif is a small design, generally worked from the center outward, such as a granny square. Motifs are frequently joined together to make a larger item such as an afghan.

BLOCKING

Many of the afghans require blocking after they are finished. This means squaring them off to the correct size and shape.

Different yarns must be treated differently, and this is why it's important to keep the labels from your yarn to refer to after the afghan has been completed. Sometimes the label gives blocking directions, but if not, you will need the information concerning what the yarn is made of.

When making a granny-square afghan, for example, you want each piece to have the correct shape. If the edges curl, for example, blocking is necessary. Each piece must be pinned down and pressed. The iron setting depends on the yarn. A cool iron must be used on synthetic materials, but natural fibers can be pressed with a warm iron. Some blocking is done by placing a damp cloth over the shaped and pinned piece. Press over the damp cloth and remove it. Then wait until the piece is dry before removing the pins. It is not advisable to press directly onto synthetic yarn without a pressing cloth between the yarn and the iron.

FRINGE

A fringed edge is a nice way to finish an afghan. Cut strands of yarn slightly more than twice the desired finished length of the fringe. Double one or more strands, depending on how thick you'd like it to be. Insert your crochet hook through the edge where the fringe is to be made and draw through the double strand or strands; draw ends through this loop and pull the ends to tighten. Continue across the piece to be fringed.

Crochet Abbreviations

beg—beginning
bet—between
ch—chain
cl—cluster
dc—double crochet
dec—decrease
dtr—double treble or triple crochet
grp—group
hdc—half double crochet
inc—increase
L—left
lp—loop
MC—main color
pat—pattern
R—right
rem—remaining
rep—repeat
rnd—round
sc—single crochet
sk—skip
sl st—slip stitch
sp—space
st—stitch
tog—together
tr—treble or triple crochet
yo—yarn over hook
*—repeat what comes after
( )—work directions in parentheses as many times as specified. For example: (dc 1, ch 1) 3 times.
[ ]—brackets are used for clarity when a section of instructions already contains a set of parentheses. Instructions in brackets are worked in the same way as instructions in parentheses.

Cross-Stitch Basics

Counted cross-stitch is not a new form of embroidery, but it has always been the most popular. Perhaps this is because it is so easy and always looks perfect.

Counted cross-stitch is basically simple, especially when worked with yarn. You need a blunt-end yarn or tapestry needle, yarn, and a charted design. The illustrations on each of the afghans in this book are created with counted cross-stitch. The background of the areas on the afghan to be cross-stitched looks like little squares, and each square is filled in with an X stitch in the color indicated on the chart.

Perhaps you've seen early American samplers dating back to Colonial days. Often cross-stitches were used to create the neat geometric rows that formed patterns, borders, numbers, letters, and sometimes scenes. Today's renewed interest in cross-stitch has fostered a modern approach to the craft and we find almost every design imaginable, from nursery figures to flowers and country symbols adapted from American folk art and quilts.

YARN

The yarn most commonly used for cross-stitch over afghans is a 3-ply Persian-type yarn. Sometimes a pattern will instruct you to use the same yarn for the embroidery that was used to make the afghan. For example, if you have used a sport weight yarn from a specific manufacturer, you can use the same yarn, in the specified colors, for the cross-stitch. However, the 3-ply yarn can be purchased in small amounts, such as 5-ounce skeins, and this is often desirable. There is also a much wider range of colors and shades of colors available in the Persian-type yarn.

For the most part, I use all 3 strands of the yarn for the cross-stitching. However, if an afghan is made of a fine baby yarn, for example, the cross-stitching looks better with only 2 strands. In this case, separate all 3 strands and use 2. Some needleworkers like to separate the strands and rejoin them even when using all 3 strands. This keeps the yarn from knotting and tangling. I did this for the first few colors on the first project I made, but quickly tired of it and simply used all 3 strands as they came off the skein because it was easier. If you cut manageable lengths of yarn, approximately 18 to 24 inches, I don't think you'll have any trouble.

NEEDLES

A blunt-end tapestry or embroidery needle, sometimes called a yarn needle, is best for cross-stitch. It will not catch or ravel the yarn the way a sharply pointed needle might. Be sure that the eye is large enough to receive all 3 strands of yarn, but not so large as to make big holes in the background material as it passes through. Needles are plastic or metal and I've found either to be acceptable.

EMBROIDERY SCISSORS

These sharp little scissors are invaluable. Keep them next to you while you work. Each time you finish a length of yarn, you'll have them handy for snipping.

How to Work Counted Cross-Stitch

THREADING THE NEEDLE

Cut the length of yarn recommended, usually about 18 to 24 inches. Double it around the eye of the needle, holding it taut and as close to the needle as possible. Slide the folded end off the needle while holding it tight. Slip the folded end through the needle eye.

FINDING THE CENTER

Some stitchers like to start their work at the center of the design, but everyone in our studio agrees that it's better to start at the bottom of the design and work up. Sometimes it's important to find the center of the design before you begin, if centering the design on the background is essential to the design. In this case, the directions will instruct you to do so.

To find your starting point, count the number of unworked squares in from one side of the chart and up from the bottom to determine the first stitch in the first row of the design. Do the same on your fabric. You are now ready to work your stitches in horizontal rows.

BEGINNING A STITCH

Do not make a knot on one end of the yarn as you would for regular sewing. Locate the first square and, from the underside of the work, weave the yarn through a couple of stitches (so it is invisible from the front), then bring your needle up through one hole of the afghan stitch as shown on page 21. Refer to this page for complete details on cross-stitching over the afghan stitch.

You will work diagonally across the row, using the same color as indicated on the chart for each project.

CROSS-STITCHING THE DESIGN

It's usually best to complete one section of the design at a time. Each time you run out of yarn, weave the last bit under a few stitches on the underside to secure the work. I must admit, my underside isn't as neat as I'd like it to be, but I can't seem to weave the ends under so they are invisible. There are expert needleworkers who do this with ease. I'm not one of them, but if you are, your work can be as lovely on the back as it is on the front.

If you're working on an area that has few stitches in each row, you might prefer to cross each stitch as you work it. With this method you have to make sure each stitch is crossed in the same direction so that the finished work looks neat.

Each hole is worked twice when the stitches are together with no spaces between. When working on isolated stitches, always complete each stitch, end the thread, and move to the next area.

BACKSTITCH

Used for outlining, this stitch looks very much like machine stitching. Stitches are even and close together and often used for stitching details, like facial features or the strings of a balloon, for example. Bring the needle up from the underside of the fabric and reinsert it a half stitch behind where the thread came through. Bring it back up a half stitch in front of this point. (See page 30 .) Continue in this way as indicated on the graph for the cross-stitch project.

CHANGING COLOR

When you are beginning a new color, weave the yarn under a few stitches on the underside of the fabric and then poke up through the appropriate hole to begin the first stitch. Do not carry one color across an area of the afghan that is more than a few stitches. Simply end the yarn by weaving under a few stitches, snip, and begin again.

Cross-Stitch Tips

Making errors, missing stitches, finding a letter inappropriately spaced, adding a row where one wasn't called for, leaving stitches unfinished—these are just some of the bothersome things that cross-stitchers put up with. To avoid some or all of these, stop to check the stitch placements now and then.

When working on a border design, for example, check often to be sure each corner is going to meet as planned. Fill in the details last, if possible. When you are working on letters, such as the alphabet in a border or a wedding date on "The Wedding Tree" (page 51), check to be sure that each letter starts and ends on the same row, if that's what is intended.

Before starting a new row, check to be sure all slants are leaning in the same direction. Try to be as consistent in your stitching pattern as possible. Take it from one who hasn't always heeded her own advice. If it becomes necessary to remove stitches, it's easier when you don't have an erratic pattern to pull out.

And last, good lighting will add years to the health of your eyes. Sunlight is wonderful lighting for doing cross-stitch, if possible. Evening seems to be when most people have leisure time to work, but daylight is really better than artificial light. So be aware that good lighting really does cut down on error.

BASIC EMBROIDERY STITCHES

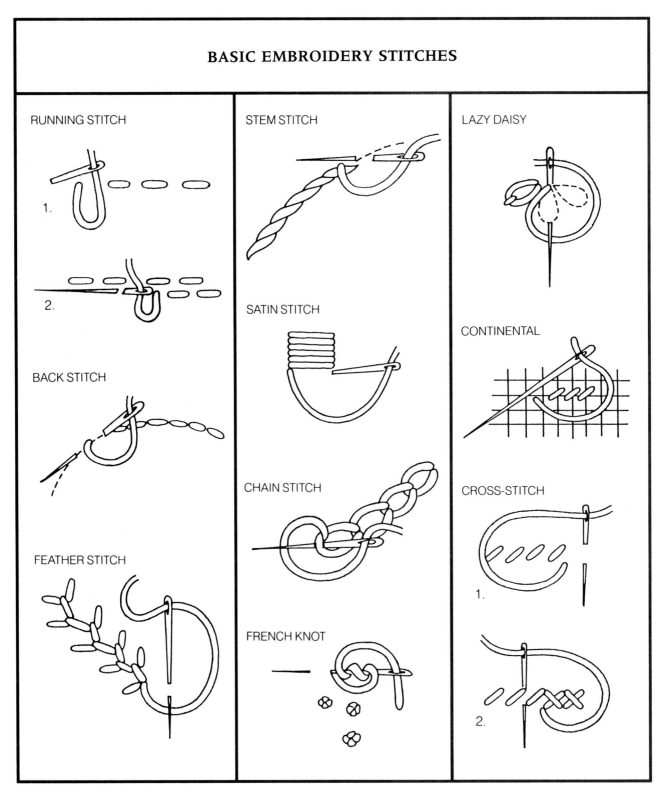

RUNNING STITCH

1.

2.

BACK STITCH

FEATHER STITCH

STEM STITCH

SATIN STITCH

CHAIN STITCH

FRENCH KNOT

LAZY DAISY

CONTINENTAL

CROSS-STITCH

1.

2.

The Afghans

American Country Afghans

*C*ountry style will probably always be with us because it's comfortable, homey, and easy to acquire. By using popular country symbols, such as hearts, houses, apple trees, and baskets, as designs on crocheted afghans, you have an irresistible country accessory. Nothing says warmth and coziness like an afghan over the back of a sofa or folded at the end of a bed.

In this chapter you'll find a wonderful wedding gift. "The Wedding Tree" will surely become a family heirloom. Consider personalizing it by embroidering the names and wedding date in the borders.

One of my favorite afghans is "An Apple a Day," with its alternating squares of apple trees and baskets of hearts.

Another country favorite is an overall, repeat tulip design in the ever-popular Shaker blue and cranberry colors, pictured on the facing page.

White hearts and houses against a royal blue background echo the theme "Home Is Where the Heart Is". Made up of granny squares, this is one of the many carry-along projects in the book.

Country Tulips

Nothing says country like pretty tulips growing in a row. Each tulip is surrounded by a geometric design, which makes it perfect for a contemporary as well as a traditional environment. This lovely afghan was designed by Ellen Boccardi for Patons Yarn. The colors used are rose, cranberry, and dark blue, which are most popular for crafting with a country flavor. The finished project is 47 × 55 inches. (See photo on overleaf.)

MATERIALS

Yarn: Patons Canadiana (3.5 oz./100 g. balls) or knitting worsted weight yarn—9 natural (MC), 2 cranberry (CC), 1 each of rose (B) and dark blue (C). *Alternate yarn choice:* Patons Super Wool (1.75 oz./50 g. balls)—20 natural (MC), 4 cranberry (CC), 2 balls each of rose (B) and dark blue (C).
Afghan hook: Susan Bates Flexible J/10 (6.5 mm) or size needed to obtain gauge.
Crochet hook: Susan Bates size J/10 (6.5 mm)
Tapestry needle

GAUGE

15 sts = 4 inches; 13 rows = 4 inches.

Directions

Using MC and the afghan hook, ch 176. Work the afghan st (see page 20) for 177 rows. Now work a row of sl st as follows: Sk the first upright bar, *sl st in next upright bar. Rep from * across. Break off and fasten.

CROSS-STITCH

Cross-stitch following the chart, beginning and ending as indicated and repeating the 22 pattern sts 7 times across. Rep the 26 pattern rows a total of 6 times. For cross-stitch directions see pages 26–29.

EDGING

With right side facing and crochet hook, join MC in a corner and work 1 rnd of reverse sc around the afghan as follows: *Swing the hook downward across the material from *left to right* and insert into next stitch to the *right,* yo and draw lp through, yo and draw through both lps on hook. Rep from * around, taking care to keep work flat. Join with sl st to first reverse sc. Break off and fasten.

⊠ CRANBERRY
■ ROSE
⊙ DARK BLUE

Perky Posies

This bright and cheerful afghan is similar to an appliquéd quilt. Each colorful square is framed with a band of white that reflects the white flowers in the alternating squares of color. Since all the flowers are white and each design is repeated, this is an easy design to cross-stitch. It is quite graphic and summery. This is also a good project for interchanging colors to suit your room decor. The white flowers would look good against any background, whether pastels or dark hues. You could even use black instead of white for the framing borders. The finished size is approximately 48 × 67 inches. Each motif measures 8½ inches square, excluding the edging.

MATERIALS

Yarn: Coats & Clark Red Heart 4-ply worsted weight acrylic (3.5 oz./ 100 g. skeins)—16 oz. white, 13 oz. orange, 12 oz. each mustard and lilac, 9 oz. pink, 1 oz. gold.
Afghan hook: 10-inch G/6 (4.5 mm) or size needed to obtain gauge.
Tapestry needle

GAUGE

9 sts = 2 inches; 7 rows = 2 inches.

Directions

BASIC SQUARE (Motif)

Using the afghan hook, ch 39. Work the afghan st (see page 20) for 31 rows. Now, work a row of sl st as follows: Sk first upright bar, *sl st in next upright bar. Rep from * across. Break off and fasten.
Motif 1: (Make 9): With lilac, follow instructions for basic square.
Motif 2: (Make 10) With orange, follow instructions for basic square.
Motif 3: (Make 9) With mustard, follow instructions for basic square.
Motif 4: (Make 7) With pink, follow instructions for basic square.
Block each motif to measure 8½ × 8½ inches. (See page 23.)

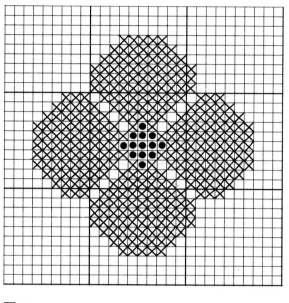

⊠ WHITE
◉ GOLD

40

EDGING

All edgings are worked with white yarn. With right side facing, attach white to upper right-hand corner.

Rnd 1: Work a rnd of sc evenly around the entire motif, making 3 sc at each corner. Join with sl st to first sc. Do not turn.

Rnd 2: Ch 1, sc in each sc around, making 3 sc in center sc of each corner. Join with sl st to first sc. Break off and fasten.

CROSS-STITCH

Mark the center upright bar of each motif to be embroidered to determine the starting point and follow the chart for placement of stitches. Cross-stitch the design in white, over the upright bars, being careful that the top strands all point in the same direction. Embroider 4 of Motif 1, 5 of Motif 2, 5 of Motif 3, and 4 of Motif 4. For cross-stitch directions see pages 26–29.

JOINING MOTIFS

Refer to photograph for position of motifs and, being careful to keep afghan sts in one direction, sew the motifs together.

BORDER

Rnd 1: With right side facing, attach the white yarn to the center sc at the upper right-hand corner, ch 1, make 3 sc in the same place, *sc in each sc across to center sc of next corner, 3 sc in corner sc. Rep from * twice more; sc in each remaining sc. Join with sl st to first sc. Break off and fasten.

An Apple a Day

The popular country designs of apple trees and hearts in a basket are repeated in alternating squares for a very graphic effect. The twelve squares done in the afghan stitch are surrounded by an airy, openwork border, making each 13 × 13 inches with a 2-inch border around the entire afghan. The finished size is approximately 46 × 63 inches.

I used Tahki's Lana wool in a natural color and it was wonderfully soft to work with. It is also washable. The cross-stitching is done with a compatible Paternayan 3-ply Persian. This project is easy to carry along, as each square is worked separately before assembling.

MATERIALS:
Yarn: *For afghan:* Tahki Imports Ltd. Lana 100% new wool (3.5 oz./100 g. skeins)—16 natural. *For cross-stitching:* Paternayan 3-ply Persian yarn (the following amounts are given in yards, not skeins)—80 yds. each of green and brown, 40 yds. red, 8 yds. tan.
Afghan hook: 10-inch K/10½ (7 mm) or size needed to obtain gauge.
Crochet hook: J/10 (6.5 mm)
Tapestry needle

GAUGE
4 sts = 1 inch; 4 rows = 1 inch. Each square contains 25 sts to the row and there must be 25 rows to accommodate each design.

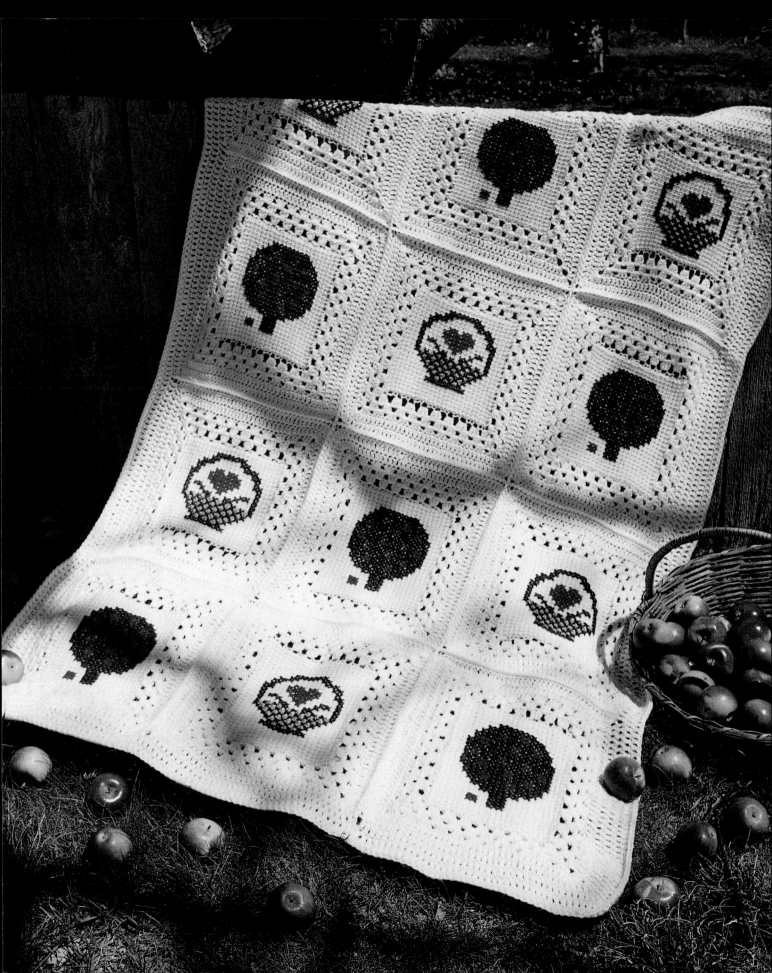

Directions

SQUARE (Make 12)

Using the afghan hook, ch 25. Work the afghan st (see page 20) for 25 rows. Do not fasten off.

Border

Change to the crochet hook. Work these rnds around the square, starting with the last lp of the afghan square at the corner.

Rnd 1: Ch 3 (first dc), 2 dc, ch 2, 3 dc in corner lp, *(sk 2 sts, 3 dc in next st) 7 times; sk 2 sts, 3 dc, ch 2, 3 dc in corner. Rep from * 2 times more, ending with (sk 2 sts, 3 dc in next st) 7 times. Join with sl st to 3rd st of ch-3. Do not turn.

Rnd 2: Sl st to corner. Ch 3 (first dc), 2 dc, ch 2, 3 dc in corner sp, *(3 dc in next sp) 8 times; 3 dc, ch 2, 3 dc in corner sp. Rep from * 2 times more, ending with (3 dc in next sp) 8 times. Join with sl st to 3rd st of ch-3. Do not turn.

Rnd 3: Work as for Rnd 2, repeating between ( ) 9 times (instead of 8).

Rnd 4: Ch 3 (1st dc). At all corners work 2 dc, ch 2, 2 dc in the corner sp. Join with sl st to 3rd st of ch-3. Do not turn.

Rnd 5: Rep Rnd 4.

Make 12 squares in this way. Don't forget to switch hook type on each square, using the afghan hook for the afghan st and the crochet hook for the surrounding border.

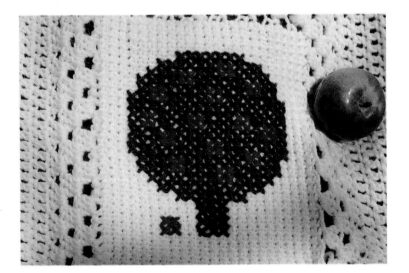

CROSS-STITCH

There are 6 squares with apple trees and 6 squares with baskets. Follow the corresponding chart for each design and be sure that each is properly centered before beginning. To do this, find the center of the design on the charts. Then find the center of each afghan panel. Count the number of plain squares from each side edge in to where the design begins. You should have the same number of unworked squares on your afghan panels. I neglected to do this on one of the squares and just began to stitch. Halfway through the cross-stitching I discovered that the design was off-center and I had to pull out all the stitches. For cross-stitch directions see pages 26–29.

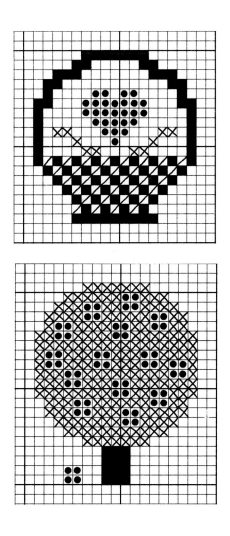

⊠ GREEN
■ BROWN
⊙ RED
◪ TAN

45

JOINING SQUARES

Beginning with an apple tree square, followed by a basket square and then another apple tree square, arrange the squares in 4 rows of 3 each, alternating the designs in each row. Crochet the squares together with sc. These squares were crocheted with wrong sides together, picking up just the inside of the dc lp to create a ridge between squares. If you prefer a flatter joining stitch, crochet with right sides together.

BORDER

Attach the yarn and work 2 rows of Rnd 4 around the entire piece. Break off and fasten. If you'd like to make the border using a contrasting color, such as the red or green, you will need 1 skein to complete the 2-inch-wide border all around.

Home Is Where the Heart Is

No two symbols are more popular in country design than the heart and the home. You find variations of these designs in quilts, stencils, cross-stitch, and knitting projects. And no wonder! These are simple, graphic shapes that are easy to create and look good on any project. The bold blue and white color scheme is just right for this granny-square afghan made by Marion Tuthill. The afghan looks like an early American quilt because of the borders and lattice strips made from small granny squares around the larger blocks containing the cross-stitch patterns. As you might imagine, this is the perfect carry-along project because all the squares are made separately and then stitched together when finished. The overall size is approximately 42 × 52 inches.

MATERIALS

Yarn: *For afghan:* Unger's Aries worsted weight acrylic/wool blend (3.5 oz./100 g. skeins)—3 each of dark blue and white, 2 light blue.
For cross-stitching: Paternayan 3-ply Persian yarn (the following amount is given in yards, not skeins)—55 yds. white.
Afghan hook: 10-inch I/9 (6 mm) or size needed to obtain gauge.
Crochet hook: H/8 (5 mm) or size needed to obtain gauge.
Tapestry needle

GAUGE

4 sts = 1 inch; 4 rows = 1 inch. (*Note:* Rows are slightly larger than sts so 24 rows counted back and forth = 7 inches.)
Motif: Embroidered afghan st square = 8 × 8 inches; small granny square = 4 × 4 inches.

Directions

There are 62 small white squares with light blue centers and 20 white squares with dark blue centers.

AFGHAN STITCH SQUARES (Make 6)

Using dark blue yarn and afghan hook, ch 34. Work the afghan st (see page 20) until the piece is 8 inches long. Now, work a row of sl st as follows: Sk the first upright bar, *sl st in next upright bar. Rep from * across to make an 8-inch square. Break off and fasten.

SMALL GRANNY SQUARES

White with Dark Blue Centers: (Make 20)

Using dark blue yarn and crochet hook, starting at the center, ch 6. Join with sl st to form ring.

Rnd 1: Ch 3 (first dc), work 2 dc in ring, (ch 1, 3 dc in ring) 3 times; ch 1. Join with sl st to 3rd st of ch-3. Break off. Do not turn.

Rnd 2: With white yarn, sl st in any ch-1 sp, ch 3 (first dc), in same sp work 2 dc, ch 1, and 3 dc (first corner); *ch 1, in next ch-1 sp work 3 dc, ch 1, and 3 dc (another corner). Rep from * 2 times more (4 corners); ch 1. Join with sl st to 3rd st of ch-3. Do not break off or turn.

Rnd 3: Ch 4 (first dc, ch 1), work (3 dc, ch 1, 3 dc in corner, ch 1, 3 dc in next ch-1 sp) 3 times omitting last dc. Join with sl st to 3rd st of ch-4. Break off.

White with Light Blue Centers: (Make 62)

Rep the 3 rnds above using light blue for Rnd 1 and white for Rnds 2 and 3.

TRIANGLE GRANNIES (Make 12 light blue and 12 dark blue)

These squares are made with 4 granny-square triangles.

Row 1: Starting at the center point, ch 5; in 5th ch from hook work 3 dc, ch 1, and 1 dc. Turn work.

Row 2: Ch 4 (first dc, ch 1), work 3 dc in first ch-1 sp; ch 1, in next ch-1 sp work 3 dc, ch 1, and 1 dc. Turn work.

Row 3: Ch 4 (first dc, ch 1), 3 dc in first ch-1 sp; ch 1, 3 dc in next ch-1 sp; ch 1, in last ch-1 sp work 3 dc, ch1, and 1 dc. Turn work.

Row 4: Ch 4 (first dc, ch 1), 3 dc in first ch-1 sp, *ch 1, 3 dc in next ch-1 sp. Rep from * to last ch-1 sp; ch 1, in last ch-1 sp work 3 dc, ch 1, and 1 dc. Turn work.

Rows 5–6: Rep Row 4. Break off and fasten.

CROSS-STITCH

Follow the charts to cross-stitch each square. You will have 2 squares of each design. Since you are working only with white yarn there are no color changes. For cross-stitch directions see pages 26–29.

TO FINISH

Arrange the squares, according to the photograph of the finished afghan, and sew together. Work 1 rnd sc with white and 1 rnd sc with dark blue around the entire piece to finish off with a nice border edge.

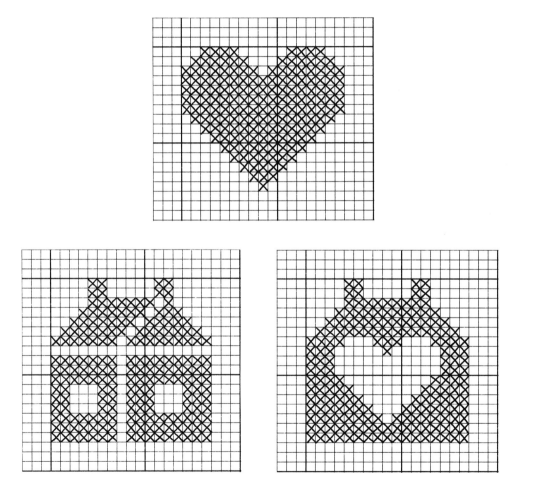

The Wedding Tree

This is a good project to make as a wedding or anniversary gift. The bride and groom are shown, standing under the family tree. This lovely afghan was designed and made by Joan Roche of Nantucket, Massachusetts. To personalize this afghan, you can cross-stitch the words *Wedded this day* and the date along one side edge in the border, with the couple's names in the border on the opposite side edge. The entire project is made with a knitting worsted, using the afghan stitch, and is 36 × 64 inches with an extra 3 inches of fringe on each end.

MATERIALS

Yarn: *For afghan:* Unger Aries worsted weight acrylic/wool blend (3.5 oz./100 g. skeins)—10 light blue. *For cross-stitching:* Paternayan 3-Ply Persian yarn (the following amounts are given in yards, not skeins)—56 yds. each of white, dark blue, and brown; 20 yds. green; 6 yds. black; 4 yds. each of light pink, dark pink, and yellow.
Crochet hook: J/10 (6.5 mm)
Tapestry needle

GAUGE

7 sts = 2 inches; 5 rows = 2 inches.

Directions

Ch 130. Starting with the 2nd lp from the hook, work the afghan st (see page 20) for 170 rows. Sc around piece, working 3 sc in each corner. Join with sl st to first sc. Break off.

CROSS-STITCH

Begin by cross-stitching the borders first. Next, find the center of the panel and cross-stitch the tree. It's important that the tree, which is the largest element, be perfectly centered so you can then add the other elements. Then, starting at the bottom edge, begin working upward, across each line. I find that it's usually easiest to do all the same color stitches at once unless the color is interrupted often.

Each person finds the best way to work on a cross-stitch project and each project presents a different problem. There isn't any universal "best" way. So, the only advice I can give is to get started and the method will evolve as you go along. This is a large project, but the design isn't complicated and the colors are limited. For cross-stitch directions see page 26–29.

TO FINISH

Cut 6–7-inch lengths of yarn for the fringe. You will use a double strand in each sc at the short ends of the afghan. For fringe directions, see page 24. For a fuller fringe, use 4 lengths of yarn to create a fringe of 8 strands. For a two-tone effect, you might like to combine white with the blue for each fringe.

☑ WHITE
☒ DARK BLUE
◉ BROWN
◩ GREEN
■ BLACK
☑ DARK PINK
◎ LIGHT PINK
⊡ YELLOW

Florentine

A Florentine design done in two colors is always striking. The olive green against a neutral background will fit with almost any decorating scheme. This project is quite large, but because it's made up of five panels it's possible to cross-stitch each section before joining them. The finished measurement is approximately 56 × 65 inches.

MATERIALS

Yarn: Coats & Clark Red Heart "Preference" 4-ply worsted weight acrylic (3.5 oz./100 g. skeins)—56 oz. cream, 25 oz. olive.
Afghan hook: 14-inch H/8 (5 mm) or size needed to obtain gauge.
Tapestry needle

GAUGE

11 sts = 3 inches; 3 rows = 1 inch.

Directions

Mark the starting chain of each panel for the lower edge of the afghan.

WIDE PANEL (Make 2)

Using cream and the afghan hook, ch 65. Work the afghan st (see page 20) for 194 rows. Now, work a row of sl st as follows: Sk the first upright bar, *sl st in next upright bar. Rep from * across. Break off and fasten.

NARROW PANEL (Make 3)

Using cream yarn and the afghan hook, ch 23. Work the afghan st for 194 rows. Finish with sl st in same manner as for wide panel.

CHART 1

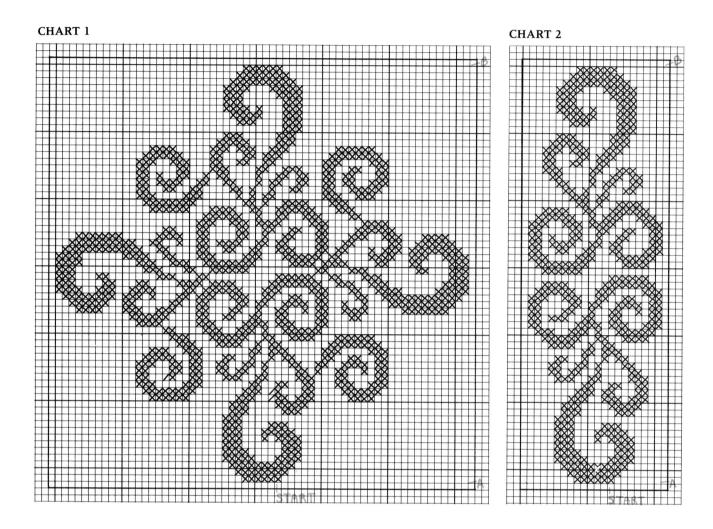

CHART 2

START

START

58

CROSS-STITCH

The cross-stitched design is worked with the olive yarn. Cross-stitches are worked over upright bars (see pages 26–29), taking care that the top strands all point in the same direction. Mark the 30th upright bar on Row 3 of wide panel for the starting point indicated on Chart 1. Starting at this point, follow Chart 1 to B. *Leave the next 2 rows free, then follow the same chart from A to B. Rep from * 1 time more.

Embroider the other wide panel in the same way. Mark the 9th upright bar on Row 3 of the narrow panel for the starting point indicated on Chart 2 and follow Chart 2 for each narrow panel in the same manner as Chart 1 was followed.

With marked edge of each panel at same end, working through both thicknesses and using olive yarn, join a narrow panel and a wide panel together with sc. Alternating narrow and wide panels, join the remaining panels together in the same manner.

BORDER

With right side facing, attach olive yarn to the upper right-hand corner.

Rnd 1: Ch1, *3 sc in corner, working along the short edge, make 21 sc across each narrow panel, 63 sc across each wide panel to next corner, 3 sc in corner, sc in end st of each row to next corner. Rep from * once more. Join with sl st to first sc—189 sc on each short edge, 195 sc on each long edge, and 3 sc in each corner. Do not turn.

Rnd 2: Sl st in 2nd of 3 corner sc, ch 1, sc in same sc,—sk 2 sc, *6 dc in next sc (shell made), sk 2 sc, sc in next sc, sk 2 sc. Rep from * around, ending with shell, sk last 2 sc. Join with sl st to first sc. Do not turn.

Rnd 3: Ch 3, 5 dc in joining, *sc in center of next shell, shell in next sc. Rep from * around, ending with sc in center of last shell. Join with sl st to 3rd st of ch-3. Break off and fasten.

Country Garden Afghans

*F*lowers are always an appealing design choice for needleworkers. Whether it's a formal garden, a basket of wildflowers, or a sprawling vine, an illustration of flowers introduces a wide range of color possibilities and gives us a chance to be creative. For example, you might like one of the illustrations, but want to try it in another color combination. You almost can't miss when it comes to flowers. Because real flowers grow in a profusion of shades of color, any variety of colors will look good together.

Some of the afghans shown in this chapter have an illustration on a center panel that is surrounded by lacy crocheted borders. Some of the illustrations are repeat patterns on long panels that are stitched together, and others are designed to fit within squares that are joined like a patchwork quilt. Many of the cross-stitched panels, by themselves, without the borders, make wonderful wall hangings. This is an ideal way to show off your handiwork.

However you choose to display or use your afghan, the floral themes will fit into any decorating style, just as real flowers do.

Forget-Me-Not

Made up of twenty-four squares, this delightful afghan is a perfect welcome to spring. Every other square has a wreath of flowers, alternating with squares that say "Forget-Me-Not." Made of acrylic yarn, this afghan is completely washable. The finished size is a comfortable 49 × 64 inches. (See photo on overleaf.) Make two extra squares, one of each design, and you'll be able to create throw pillows for a pretty ensemble. Each pillow is 11 × 12 inches.

MATERIALS

Yarn: 4-ply worsted weight acrylic—45 oz. white, 21 oz. pink, 3½ oz. each of light blue and yellow, 3 oz. green.
Crochet hook: J/10 (6.5 mm) or size needed to obtain gauge.
Tapestry needle
Polyester filling for pillows

GAUGE

7 sc = 2 inches, 4 rows = 1 inch.

Directions for Afghan

MOTIF (Make 24)

With white, ch 29.
Row 1: Sc in 2nd ch from hook and in each chain across—28 sc.
Row 2: Ch 1, turn. Sk first st, sc in next and in each st across.
Row 3: Ch 1, turn. Sk first st, sc in next and in each st across. Sc in turning ch. Rep Row 3 until there are 37 rows. Break off and fasten.

EDGING

With right side facing, join pink in a corner of the motif.
Rnd 1: Sc evenly around the entire outer edge, working 3 sc in each corner. Join with sl st to the first sc. Do not turn.
Rnd 2: Ch 1, sc in each stitch around, working 3 sc in center sc of each corner. Join with sl st to first sc. Do not turn.
Rnd 3: Rep Rnd 2. Break off and fasten.

CROSS-STITCH

You will cross-stitch 12 motifs with the flower design shown on Chart 1 and 12 motifs with the Forget-Me-Not design shown on Chart 2. Locate the center of the motif and count up from the bottom on the chart to determine where you will begin the cross-stitching. Work from the bottom up, across each line with 1 color at a time as indicated on the chart. You will be working 1 cross-stitch over each sc. For cross-stitch directions see pages 26–29.

JOINING MOTIFS

With right sides facing, and using pink, sew through outside lps only to join motifs together, arranging as shown in photograph.

BORDER

With right side facing, join pink at a corner. Work 2 rnds of sc evenly around the entire outer edge, making 3 sc in each corner. Break off and fasten.

Directions for Pillow

MOTIF (Make 2 for each pillow)

Work as for afghan motif. Break off and fasten.

MOTIF EDGING

Work as for afghan motifs but with 5 rnds of sc (rather than 3).

CROSS-STITCH

Cross-stitch 1 motif following Chart 1 and another following Chart 2. For cross-stitch directions see pages 26–29. Plain motifs are used for the backing of each pillow.

TO FINISH

With right sides facing and using pink, sew through outside lps only to join 3 sides of a cross-stitched motif and a plain motif together, leaving the last side open. Turn right side out. Fill with stuffing to desired firmness. Stitch the opening closed with overcast st.

CHART 1

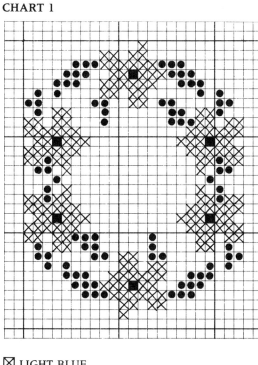

CHART 2

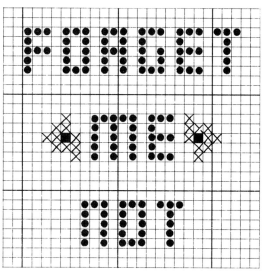

 LIGHT BLUE
YELLOW
GREEN

A Bouquet of Roses

This pretty, scalloped-edge lap throw was designed to go in a bedroom. However, it would be at home in almost any blue and white setting. The center panel is worked in the afghan stitch over which you'll cross-stitch the rose bouquet held together with a graceful ribbon bow. To "frame" your still life, crochet a scalloped, lacy border all around and trim with blue satin ribbon tied in bows at each corner. The center panel is 30 × 42 inches and the border is 6 inches deep, for a finished project that measures 42 × 54 inches.

MATERIALS

Yarn: *For afghan:* Tahki Imports Ltd. Lana 100% new wool (3.5 oz./100 g. skeins)—8 natural; 6 yards ¼-inch-wide blue satin ribbon. *For cross-stitching:* Paternayan 3-ply Persian yarn (the following amounts are given in yards, not skeins)—35 yds. cobalt blue, 56 yds. loden green, 57 yds. light green, 31 yds. deep rose, 24 yds. light rose, 12 yds. each of pink and yellow.

Afghan hook: 14-inch K/10½ (7 mm) or size needed to obtain gauge.

Crochet hook: I/9 (6 mm) or size needed to obtain gauge.

Tapestry needle

GAUGE

3 sts = 1 inch; 3 rows = 1 inch.

short edge to corner, 3 sc in corner, 125 sc across long edge to corner. Rep from * 1 time more. Join with sl st to first sc. Do not turn.

Rnd 2: Sl st in 2nd of 3 corner sc, ch 5, in same st dc, ch 2, dc (corner made); *ch 1, sk next st, dc in next st to corner, ch 1, sk next st; in corner st (dc, ch 2) 2 times, dc. Rep from * 2 times more. Ch 1, sk next st, dc in next st to first corner made, ch 1, sk next st. Join with sl st to 3rd st of ch-5. Do not turn.

Rnd 3: Ch 3, dc in same sp, 2 dc in next sp, ch 3 (corner made), *2 dc in each sp to corner, ch 3. Rep from * 2 times more. Work 2 dc in each remaining sp of last side. Join with sl st to 3rd st of ch-3 (96 dc at short edges; 132 dc at long edges). Do not turn.

Rnd 4: Ch 3 (first dc), work 1 dc in each dc. At all corners work 3 dc, ch 3, 3 dc in corner sp. Join with sl st to 3rd st of ch-3. Do not turn.

Rnds 5–7: Rep Rnd 4 (120 dc at short edges; 156 dc at long edges).

Rnd 8: Sl st to 7th dc before corner, sc bet 6th and 7th dc, ch 3, sc bet 3rd and 4th dc (*from st just worked, now and for rest of rnd*), 9 tr in corner sp (corner made), sc bet 3rd and 4th dc, (ch 3, sc bet 3rd and 4th dc) 2 times; [*6 tr bet 3rd and 4th dc, sc bet 3rd and 4th dc, (ch 3, sc bet 3rd and 4th dc) 2 times. Rep from * to corner, 9 tr in corner sp]. Rep between [ ] 2 times more. **Sc bet 3rd and 4th dc, (ch 3, sc bet 3rd and 4th dc) 2 times, 6 tr bet 3rd and 4th dc. Rep from ** across last side, ending with sc bet 3rd and 4th dc, ch 3. Join with sl st to first sc. Do not turn.

Rnd 9: Ch 1, sc in first sc, *2 tr in next sc, 2 tr in each tr, 2 tr in next sc, sc in next sc. Rep from * around, ending with 2 tr in next sc, 2 tr in each tr, 2 tr in next sc. Join with sl st to first sc. Break off and fasten.

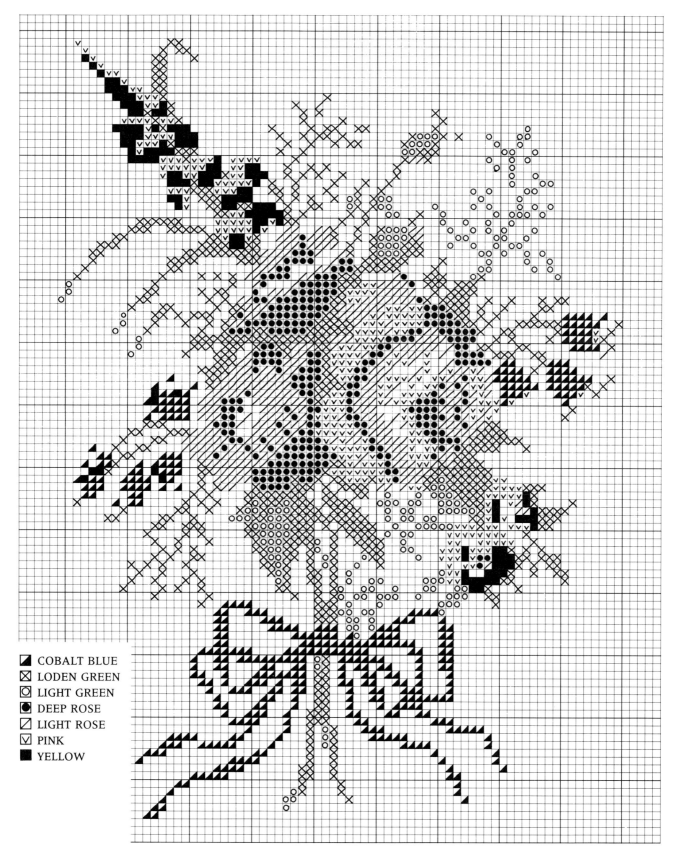

COBALT BLUE
LODEN GREEN
LIGHT GREEN
DEEP ROSE
LIGHT ROSE
PINK
YELLOW

71

Weave the satin ribbon in and out around the panel and tie a bow at each corner.

72

Floral Vines

This exquisite design was introduced by the Bernat Yarn and Craft Company in 1962. It is an adaptation of an antique tapestry bell-pull found in a Danish mansion, and was extremely popular. I tried to find the original afghan in order to include it, but the company had long ago lost track of it. And then a funny thing happened. While Jon was meeting with one of our crocheters, Joan Roche, she showed him an afghan she had started but never finished. It was this exact afghan from the Bernat pattern, which she had saved. Joan agreed to finish it for the book and decided to simplify the design, keeping the center panel plain, with the cross-stitch design on the two outside panels only. The center panel is slightly narrower than the other two, making the afghan a bit more manageable.

Made with Bernat Sesame wool, this is a warm winter afghan. The finished size is approximately 64 × 72 inches without the fringe.

MATERIAL

Yarn: *For afghan:* Bernat Sesame worsted weight wool (3.5 oz./ 100 g. skeins)—18 natural (MC), 7 light olive green (A), 2 dark olive green (B). *For cross-stitching:* DMC Floralia 3-ply Persian yarn (the following amounts are given in yards, not skeins)—120 yds. light green; 231 yds. medium green; 108 yds. dark green; 60 yds. bronze; 26 yds. each of yellow, fuschia, and light fuschia; 33 yds. each of pink, and terra cotta; 42 yds. berry red; and 17 yds. dark brown.
Afghan hook: 14-inch Bernat Aero G/6 (4.5 mm) or size needed to obtain gauge.
Crochet hook: Bernat Aero G/6 (4.5 mm)
Bernat Aero Tapestry needle

GAUGE

5 sts = 1 inch; 9 rows = 2 inches.

Directions

WIDE SIDE PANELS (Make 2)

Using MC and the afghan hook, ch 79. Work in the afghan st (see page 20) for 313 rows. Now, work a row of sl st as follows: Sk first upright bar, *sl st in next upright bar. Rep from * across. Break off and fasten.

CENTER PANEL (Make 1)

Using MC and the afghan hook, ch 40. Work in the afghan st for 313 rows. Work a row of sl st as for wide panel. Break off and fasten.

NARROW PANELS (Make 4)

Using A and the afghan hook, ch 21. Work in the afghan st for 313 rows. Work a row of sl st as for wide panel. Break off and fasten.

CROSS-STITCH

Following the chart and starting 5 rows from the top, begin at A and work to B, then work between C and D, then repeat between A and B, omitting the lower left flowers (right of D) and the leaf below the rose stem at the lower edge of the afghan. For cross-stitch directions see pages 26–29.

TO FINISH

Arrange the panels so you start and end with a narrow green panel and the green panels alternate with the wide cream panels. With wrong sides facing, using the crochet hook and B, sc all panels together. Work 1 rnd of sc around the entire outer edge of the afghan.

FRINGE

Cut strands of yarn 11 inches long. Matching colors, start with dark green, knot 3 strands of yarn in every 4th st along the short ends of the afghan, having 1 knot of dark green at each joining of the panels. Separate strands of 2 adjoining fringes and knot together.

FLORAL VINES: BOTTOM HALF

◯ LIGHT GREEN	▣ PINK	
⊠ MEDIUM GREEN	☑ TERRA COTTA	
◉ DARK GREEN	▲ BERRY RED	
☑ BRONZE	■ DARK BROWN	
⊡ YELLOW		
◪ FUCHSIA		
⬚ LIGHT FUCHSIA		

narrow, joining borders that sport evenly spaced picot designs. This is a project you'll enjoy working on because it's easy to do yet challenging enough to be interesting. The finished afghan is 60 × 68 inches.

MATERIALS

Yarn: Brunswick Windrush worsted weight acrylic (3.5 oz./100 g. skeins)—13 ecru (MC); 1 each of light ivy, green, light blue, medium blue, lilac; 27 yds. goldenrod; 19 yds. brown; 16 yds. pink; 3 yds. burnt orange. *Alternate yarn choice:* Brunswick Germantown worsted weight wool.
Afghan hook: 14-inch H/8 (5 mm) or size needed to obtain gauge.
Crochet hook: H/8 (5 mm)
Tapestry needle

GAUGE

4 sts = 1 inch; 3 rows = 1 inch.

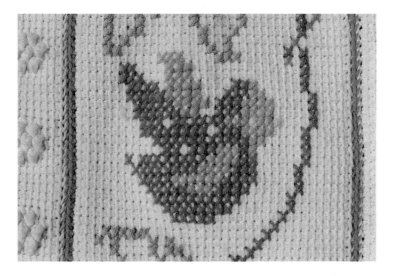

Tip: To help you keep track of both rows and embroidery placement, run a colored thread into the end of every 10th row.

NARROW PANEL (Make 4)

Refer to the chart for picot placement. Using the afghan hook, ch 11. Work the afghan st for 5 rows.

Row 6: Work 4 afghan sts (loop on hook always counts as first st), insert hook under next bar and draw up lp, ch 4 (picot), work 1 afghan st, 1 picot, 4 afghan sts. *Note:* On the 2nd half of all picot rows, work top ch of each picot as 1 lp. Always count sts at the end of the 2nd half of a row.

Row 7: Work 3 afghan sts, 1 picot, 1 afghan st, 1 picot, 1 afghan st, 1 picot, 3 afghan sts.

Row 8: Rep Row 6. *Work 7 rows of basic afghan st, then rep Rows 6 through 8. Rep from * 18 times more, ending with 5 rows of afghan st (203 rows). Finish with sl st in same manner as for wide panel.

CROSS-STITCH

Follow Wide Panel Chart 1 for 3 of the wide panels, and Wide Panel Chart 2 for the other panels. To work the charts begin with the bottom of the chart, work the first 10 rows, then rep Rows 1 through 92 twice. End by working the last 9 rows (203 rows). Work all cross-stitches slanting in the same direction. For cross-stitch directions see pages 26–29.

TO FINISH

Using the crochet hook and lilac, work 1 row of sc across each long edge of each wide panel. With right sides facing and MC, sew long edges of Wide Panel 1 and a narrow panel together, catching only the outside lp of all edge stitches and being sure the ends are even. In the same manner, sew Wide Panel 2, then a narrow panel, then Wide Panel 1, a narrow panel, Wide Panel 2, a narrow panel, and finally Wide Panel 1.

Using the crochet hook and lilac, sc across both short edges. Then, with MC, sc around the entire afghan to finish.

WIDE PANEL CHART 1 WIDE PANEL CHART 2 NARROW PICOT PANEL

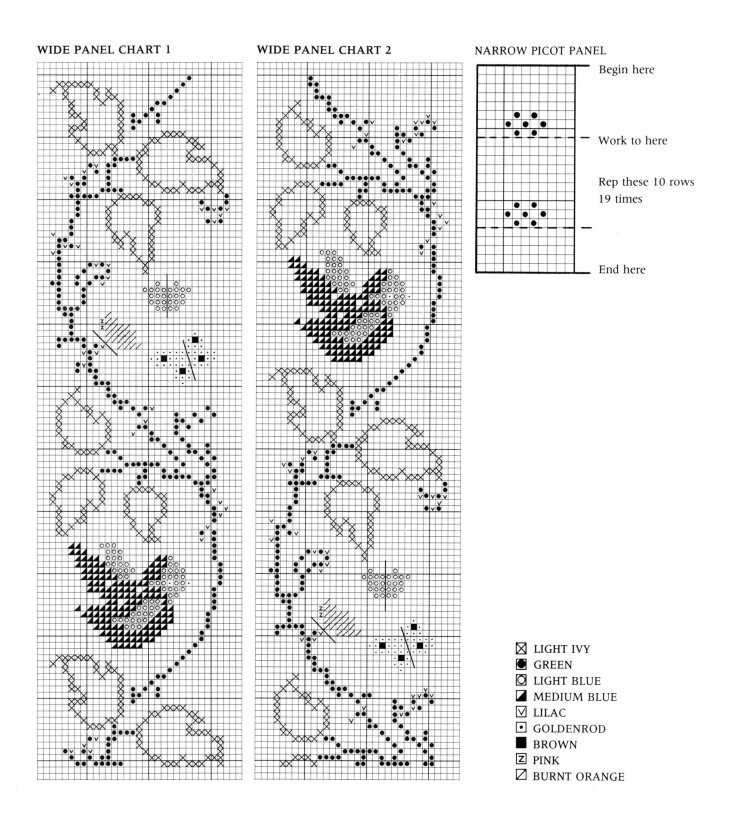

Begin here

Work to here

Rep these 10 rows
19 times

End here

⊠ LIGHT IVY
◉ GREEN
◎ LIGHT BLUE
◪ MEDIUM BLUE
▽ LILAC
⊡ GOLDENROD
■ BROWN
☑ PINK
◩ BURNT ORANGE

81

wall hanging as well as a delightful lap throw. The basket of flowers is a challenging design to cross-stitch, but the finished result is well worth the time spent. I particularly enjoyed embroidering this project.

My mother, Ruth Linsley, and I worked together. She first crocheted the background panel; I did the cross-stitch, then gave it back to her to create the borders. This is a good way to work jointly on a project if one person prefers the cross-stitching, while another finds the crochet work to be a more satisfying activity.

The finished afghan is approximately 45 inches square.

MATERIALS

Yarn: *For afghan:* Bernat Berella "4" worsted weight acrylic (3.5 oz./100 g. skeins)—3 each of white, pink, and burgundy. *For cross-stitching:* DMC Floralia 3-ply Persian yarn (the following amounts are given in yards, not skeins)—37 yds. blue, 24 yds. dark green, 44 yds. light green, 14 yds. yellow, 8 yds. purple, 18 yds. dark pink, 8 yds. light pink
Afghan hook: 14-inch H/8 (5 mm) or size needed to obtain gauge.
Crochet hook: H/8 (5 mm)
Tapestry needle

GAUGE

4 sts = 1 inch; 3¼ rows = 1 inch.

Follow the chart to cross-stitch the basket of flowers. For cross-stitch directions see pages 26–29.

INSIDE BORDER

Using the crochet hook and pink, join yarn in a corner.

Rnd 1: Work a rnd of sc evenly around the piece, working 2 sc in each corner. Join with sl st to first sc. Do not turn.

Rnd 2: Ch 1, work 1 sc in each sc. At all corners, work 2 sc in each of the 2 corner sc. Join with sl st to first sc. Do not turn.

Rnd 3: Ch 3 (first dc), work 1 dc in each sc. At all corners, work 2 dc in each of the 2nd and 3rd sc of the 4 corner sc. Join with sl st to 3rd st of ch-3. Do not turn.

Rnd 4: Ch 3 (first dc), work 1 dc in each dc. At all corners, work 3 dc bet the 2nd and 3rd dc of the 4 corner dc. Join with sl st to 3rd st of ch-3. Do not turn.

Rnds 5–7: Ch 3 (first dc), work 1 dc in each dc. At all corners, work 3 dc in the 2nd of the 3 corner dc. Join with sl st to 3rd st of ch-3. Do not turn.

Rnd 8: Ch 3 (first dc), work 1 dc in each dc. At all corners, work 2 dc in each of the 3 corner dc. Join with sl st to 3rd st of ch-3. Do not turn.

Rnd 9: Ch 3 (first dc), work 1 dc in each dc. At all corners, work 2 dc in the 3rd dc of the 6 corner dc, 2 dc bet 3rd and 4th dc, and 2 dc in 4th dc. Join with sl st to 3rd st of ch-3. Do not turn.
Rep Rnd 9 until the pink border is 5 inches. Break off and fasten.

OUTSIDE BORDER

Using the crochet hook and burgundy, join yarn bet the 3rd and 4th dc of the 6 corner dc of last rnd.

Rnd 1: Ch 4 (first tr), 2 tr in same sp, 2 sc in each of next 2 sts, [*tr in each of next 3 sts, 2 sc in each of next 2 sts. Rep from * to corner; work 3 tr bet 3rd and 4th dc of 6 corner dc]. Rep bet [ ] 2 times more. Work 2 sc in each of next 2 sts, **tr in each of next 3 sts, 2 sc in each of next 2 sts. Rep from ** across last side. Join with sl st

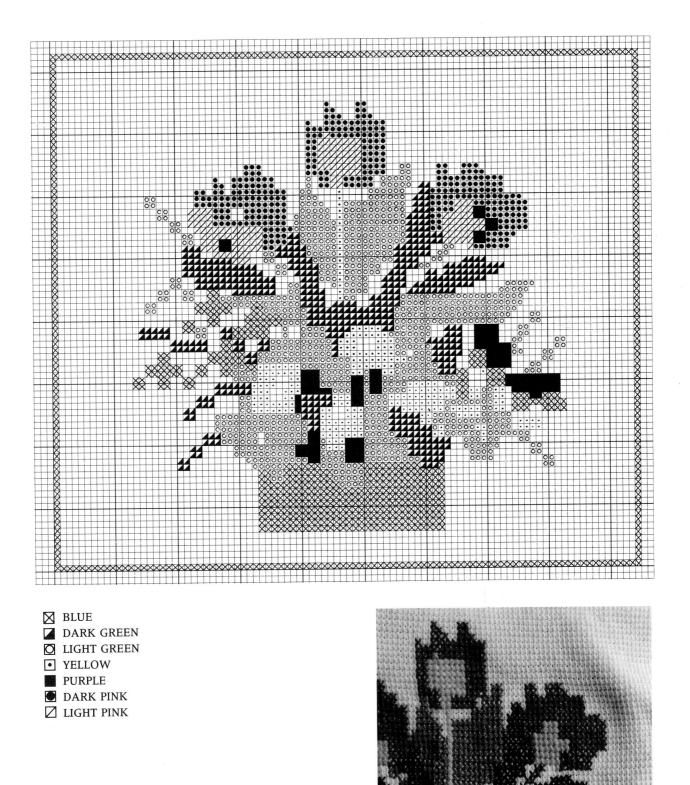

⊠ BLUE
◩ DARK GREEN
◎ LIGHT GREEN
⊡ YELLOW
■ PURPLE
◉ DARK PINK
⧄ LIGHT PINK

85

Rnd 3: Sl st into ch-6 sp, ch 3 (first dc), 4 dc in same sp, ch 1, sk next sc, *5 dc in next ch-6 sp, ch 1, sk next sc. Rep from * around. Join with sl st to 3rd st of ch-3. Do not turn.

Rnd 4: Ch 3 (first dc), dc in next dc, 2 dc in next dc (inc made), dc in next 2 dc, sc in next ch-1 sp, *dc in next 2 dc, 2 dc in next dc (inc made), dc in next 2 dc, sc in next ch-1 sp. Rep from * around. Join with sl st to 3rd st of ch-3. Do not turn.

Rnd 5: Ch 3 (first dc), dc in next 2 dc, 2 dc in next dc (inc made), dc in next 2 dc, sc in next sc, *dc in next 3 dc, 2 dc in next dc (inc made), dc in next 2 dc, sc in next sc. Rep from * around. Join with sl st to 3rd st of ch-3. Do not turn.

Rnd 6: Ch 3 (first dc), dc in next 6 dc, ch 3, sk next sc, *dc in next 7 dc, ch 3, sk next sc. Rep from * around. Join with sl st to 3rd st of ch-3. Do not turn.

Rnd 7: Ch 3 (first dc), dc in next 6 dc, sc in next ch-3 sp, *dc in next 7 dc, sc in next ch-3 sp. Rep from * around. Join with sl st to 3rd st of ch-3. Do not turn.

Rnd 8: Ch 3 (first dc), dc in next 6 dc, sc in next sc, *dc in next 7 dc, sc in next sc. Rep from * around. Join with sl st to 3rd st of ch-3. Do not turn.

Rnd 9: Ch 1, *sc in next 7 dc, 3 tr in next sc. Rep from * around. Join with sl st to first sc. Break off and fasten.

Gingham and Daisies

Who can resist a perky yellow gingham afghan dotted with springtime daisies? The lacy white scalloped edging adds just the right accent all around this 51 × 66–inch afghan. Not only good-looking, this is a warm and easy-to-care-for blanket made of knitting worsted. It would be at home in a den, at the end of a bed, or folded over the living room sofa.

MATERIALS

Yarn: Brunswick Windrush worsted weight acrylic; Classic or Heatherblend are interchangeable yarns (3.5 oz./100 g. skeins)—10 white, 4 each of light goldenrod and goldenrod, 1 each of dark goldenrod and ivy green.
Afghan hook: 10-inch J/10 (6.5 mm) or size needed to obtain gauge.
Crochet hook: J-10 (6.5 mm)
Tapestry needle

GAUGE

4 sts = 1 inch; 7 rows = 2 inches. **Motif:** Each square is 7½ × 7¼ inches before border.

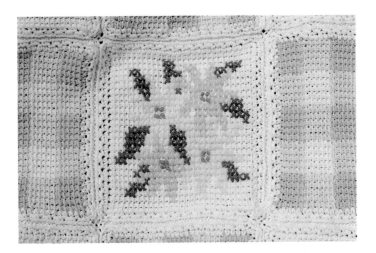

Directions

DAISY SQUARES (Make 24)

Using the afghan hook and white, ch 30 and work in the afghan st (see page 20) for 25 rows. Now, work a row of sl st as follows: Sk the first upright bar, *sl st in next upright bar. Rep from * across. Break off and fasten.

GINGHAM SQUARES (Make 24)

Note: Divide goldenrod, light goldenrod, and white into small balls— 3 of each of the goldenrods and 2 of white.

Using the afghan hook and goldenrod, ch 5, *join light goldenrod and ch 5; join goldenrod and ch 5. Rep from * 1 time more; end by making 1 more goldenrod ch. The 6th ch of each of the first 5 color blocks is made when the new color is drawn through the ch.

Rows 1–5: Working in the afghan st, make sts in the same colors as the initial ch, until 5 rows have been completed.

Note: When changing colors in the first half of a row of afghan sts, bring the new color under the strand of the old color, then continue. In the 2nd half of the row, draw through lps with the same color used for the st in the first half. Break off each color after Row 5, leaving about a 3-inch end. Refer to Chart A.

Rows 6–10: Working in the same manner as for the first 5 rows, make the first 6 sts in light goldenrod, *the next 6 sts in white, the next 6 sts in light goldenrod. Rep from * once more.

Rows 11–20: Rep Rows 1–10.

Rows 21–25: Rep Rows 1–5. Work a sl st row in the same manner as for the daisy square, keeping to the color sequence of the last row worked.

CROSS-STITCH

Following Chart B, embroider the flowers using cross-stitch, except for the center of each flower, which is worked with French knots. For cross-stitch directions see pages 26–29.

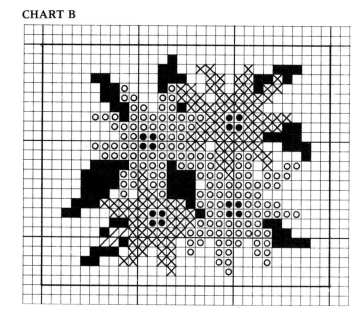

CHART B

BORDER

With right side facing, using crochet hook and white, join yarn at a corner.

Rnd 1: Sc evenly around the entire outer edge, working 3 sc at each corner. Join with sl st to first sc. Do not turn.

Rnd 2: Ch 1, sc in 2nd of 3 corner sc, *ch 1, sk next st, 2 sc in next st. Rep from * around, ending with ch 1 at all corners, ch 1, sc in 2nd of 3 corner sc, ch 1. Join with sl st to first sc. Break off and fasten.

Note: You may have to make adjustments for the corners to work out properly. Make adjustments by working 2 sc into separate sts (instead of same st).

JOINING SQUARES

Arrange the daisy squares and the gingham squares in a checkerboard pattern so there are 8 vertical rows with 6 squares across each row. With right sides facing and using white, sew the squares together, catching only the outside lps of all sts.

OUTSIDE BORDER

With right side facing, using crochet hook and white, join yarn in the ch-1 sp just to the left of a corner. Ch 1, sc in same sp, *sk 2 sc, 5 dc in next ch-1 sp, sk 2 sc, sc in next ch-1 sp. Rep from * around, working a sc or 5 dc into each seam end. At all corners, work a sc in the first corner ch-1 sp, 7 dc in the corner sc, and a sc in the last corner ch-1 sp. Join with sl st to first sc. Break off and fasten.

Note: You may have to make adjustments for the corners to work out properly. Make adjustments by working bet 2 sc (instead of skipping).

the holidays. It will be treasured by whoever is lucky enough to receive it.

The design, from the Wm. Unger Company, has a Scandinavian feeling, with the cross-stitch design of holly leaves and berries worked in the center panel and surrounded by red and white granny squares. The assembly is done after all the sections are completed, which makes this a good carry-along project. The green triangles that form the borders are reminiscent of early country quilt patterns. The finished afghan is 56 × 56 inches.

MATERIALS

Yarn: Unger Fluffy worsted weight acrylic (1.75 oz./50 g. balls)—14 white (A), 3 green (B), and 2 red (C). *Alternate yarn choice:* Unger Roly Poly (3.5 oz./100 g. balls)—9 white (A), 2 green (B), 2 red (C).
Afghan hook: I/9 (6 mm) or size needed to obtain gauge.
Crochet hook: I/9 (6 mm)
Tapestry needle

GAUGE

4 sts = 1 inch; 7 rows = 2 inches; each square = 7½ inches.

Do not break off.

Edging: Ch 1, sc evenly around entire outer edge, working 3 sc at each corner, making sure that opposite sides have the same number of sts. Join with a sl st to first sc. Break off and fasten.

CROSS-STITCH

Follow the chart and cross-stitch design motif with B. Work French knots where indicated with C. For cross-stitch directions see pages 26–29.

⊠ GREEN
◉ RED (French Knots)

WEDGE STITCH EDGING

First Side

Row 1: With right side facing and using crochet hook, join B in a corner st of center panel; sc in same place; *ch 6, sc in 2nd ch from hook, dc in next ch, tr in next 2 chs, dtr in last ch (wedge st made), sk 1⅛ inches along edge, sc in next st on edge (make sure work lies flat). Rep from * across, working 16 wedge sts to next corner; end with sc in corner. Change to A, ch 5, and turn.

Row 2: Sl st in tip of first wedge st; *working along opposite side of wedge st base ch, sc in base of sc, dc in base of dc, tr in base of each tr, dtr in base of dtr, sl st in tip of next wedge st. Rep from * across, ending with dtr in base of last dtr. Break off and fasten.

Second Side

Work as for first side along opposite edge of center panel. Break off and fasten.

Third Side

Row 1: With right side facing, join B in 5th ch of A turning ch of previous side; sc in same place; ch 6, work a wedge st in the ch-6; sc in corner of center panel; work 16 wedge sts across to next corner of center panel; sc in corner; work another wedge st; end with sc in top of A dtr at opposite edge. Change to A, ch 5, and turn.

Row 2: Work as for first side. Break off and fasten.

Fourth Side

Work as for third side along remaining edge of center panel.

BORDER

Rnd 1: With right side facing and using crochet hook, join A in a corner of wedge st edging; ch 1, 3 sc in same place for corner; work 89 sc across to next corner (about 5 sc across each wedge st section); 3 sc in corner. Rep from * 2 times more, ending with 89 sc across last side. Join with sl st to first sc. Do not turn.

Rnd 2: Ch 3 (first dc), *5 dc in 2nd of 3 corner sc, dc in each st to next corner. Rep from * around. Join with a sl st to 3rd st of ch-3. Do not turn.

Rnd 3: Ch 3 (first dc), dc in each st to corner; *5 dc in 3rd of 5 corner dc, dc in next 4 dc, (ch 1, sk next st, dc in next st, ch 1, sk next st, dc in next 4 sts) 13 times. Rep from * around, ending with 1 dc (instead of 4). Join with sl st to 3rd st of ch-3. Do not turn.

Rnd 4: Ch 3 (first dc), dc in each st to corner; *5 dc in 3rd of 5 corner dc, dc in each dc and ch 1 over each ch-1 sp to next corner. Rep from * around. Join with sl st to 3rd st of ch-3. Do not turn.

95

Work both rows of wedge st edging on all 4 sides as before, working 20 wedge sts on first and second sides and 22 wedge sts on third and fourth sides. With right side facing and using A, work a rnd of sc evenly around entire outer edge, working 3 sc in each corner, making sure opposite sides have the same number of sts. Break off and fasten.

SOLID SQUARES (Make 12)

Rnd 1: Starting at center with crochet hook and A, ch 4; 2 dc in the 4th ch from hook, (ch 3, 3 dc in same ch) 3 times; ch 3. Join with sl st to top of beg ch. Do not turn.

Rnd 2: Sl st to next corner ch-3 sp; ch 3 (first dc), in same sp work 2 dc, ch 3, 3 dc; *in next corner ch-3 sp work 3 dc, ch 3, 3 dc. Rep from * around. Join with sl st to 3rd st of ch-3. Do not turn.

Rnd 3: Sl st to next corner ch-3 sp; ch 3 (first dc), in same sp work 2 dc, ch 3, 3 dc; *sk next 3 dc, 3 dc bet last 3 dc and next 3 dc; sk next 3 dc, 3 dc, ch 3, 3 dc in next corner ch-3 sp. Rep from * around, ending with 3 dc bet 3-dc grps. Join with sl st to 3rd st of ch-3. Do not turn.

Rnd 4-5: Work as for Rnd 3, making two 3-dc grps bet corners on Rnd 4 and three 3-dc grps bet corners on Rnd 5.

Rnd 6: Sl st to next corner ch-3 sp; ch 3 (first dc), 2 dc, ch 3, 3 dc in same sp; *(sk 3 dc, dc bet last 3-dc grp and next 3-dc grp, tr in last dc of 3-dc grp 2 rnds below, 2 dtr in center dc of 3-dc grp 3 rnds below, tr in center dc of next 3-dc grp 2 rnds below, dc bet 3-dc grps behind dtr and next 3-dc grp) 2 times; sk 3 dc, in corner ch-3 sp work 3 dc, ch 3, 3 dc. Rep from * 2 times more, ending with rep bet ( ) 2 times on last side, sk 3 dc. Join with sl st to 3rd st of ch-3. Do not turn.

Rnd 7: Ch 1, sc in each st around, working 3 sc in each corner ch-3 sp. Join with sl st to first sc. Break off and fasten.

TWO-COLOR SQUARES (Make 12)

Rnd 1: Starting at the center with crochet hook and C, work as for solid square. Break off and fasten.

Rnd 2: Join A in a ch-3 sp; ch 1, sc in same sp; (ch 4, 3 sc in next ch-3 sp) 3 times; ch 4, 2 sc in first ch-3 sp. Join with sl st to first sc. Do not turn.

Rnd 3: Sl st to next ch-4 sp; ch 3 (first dc), in same sp work 2 dc, ch 3, 3 dc (first corner made); *in next ch-4 sp work 3 dc, ch 3, 3 dc (corner made). Rep from * around. Join with sl st to 3rd st of ch-3. Do not turn.

Rnd 4: Ch 3 (first dc), 2 dc over joining; *work corner as for Rnd 3 in next ch-3 sp; 3 dc bet next two 3-dc grps. Rep from * around, ending with a corner. Join with sl st to 3rd st of ch-3. Break off and fasten.

Rnd 5: Join C in a corner ch-3 sp; ch 3 (first dc), complete full corner in same sp; *(2 dc bet next two 3-dc grps; 3 dtr in center sc 2 rnds below; 2 dc bet 3-dc grp behind dtr and next 3-dc grp); complete a full corner in next ch-3 sp. Rep from * 2 times more, ending with rep bet ( ) 1 time on last side. Join with sl st to 3rd st of ch-3.

Rnd 6: Sl st to next corner ch-3 sp; ch 3 (first dc) and complete a full corner in same sp. (*3 dc bet next 3-dc grp and next 2-dc grp; 3 dc in center dtr; 3 dc bet next 2-dc grp and next 3-dc grp); complete a full corner in next ch-3 sp. Rep from * 2 times more, ending with rep bet ( ) 1 time on last side. Join with sl st to 3rd st of ch-3. Break off and fasten.

Rnd 7: Join A in corner ch-3 sp; ch 3 (first dc), complete a full corner in same sp, (*sk next 3 dc, dc bet last 3-dc grp and next 3-dc grp; tr in last dc of next 3-dc grp 2 rnds below, 2 dtr in center dc of next 3-dc grp 3 rnds below, tr in last dc of 2-dc grp 2 rnds below, dc bet 3-dc grp behind dtr and next 3-dc grp, sk next 3 dc, dc in sp bet last 3-dc grp and next 3-dc grp, tr in last dc of 2-dc grp 2 rnds below, 2 dtr in center dc of next 3-dc grp 3 rnds below, tr in first dc of next 3-dc grp 2 rnds below, dc bet 3-dc grp behind dtr and next 3-dc grp); complete a full corner in next ch-3 sp. Rep from * 2 times more, ending with rep between ( ) 1 time on last side. Join with sl st to 3rd st of ch-3. Do not turn.

Rnd 8: Ch 1, sc in each st around, working 3 sc in each corner ch-3 sp. Join with sl st to first sc. Break off and fasten.

JOINING SQUARES

Catching outside lps only, sew squares together, alternating solid and two-color squares to form a frame with 5 squares on each side and a two-color square at each corner. Sew frame to edges of center panel as shown in photograph.

in top of each wedge st and skipping the sc bet wedge sts. Join with sl st to first sc. Break off and fasten.

POINSETTIA (Make 4)

With crochet hook and C, ch 4. Join with sl st to form a ring. *Ch 8, sl st in 2nd ch from hook, sc in next 2 chs, dc in next 2 chs, sc in next ch, leave last ch unworked; ch 1, working along opposite side of beg ch work sc in same ch as last sc, dc in next 2 chs, sc in next 2 chs, sl st in next ch, sl st in first sl st of opposite side (petal made); ch 1, working along center of petal and holding yarn at back of work, sl st to opposite end (be sure work is flat); end with sl st in first ch of beg ch, sl st in ring. Rep from * 4 times more. Break off and fasten. Sew a flower at each corner of border section as shown in photograph.

Wildflower Vine

The center panel of this afghan is filled with a graceful vine of flowers sprouting in all directions. The surrounding borders reflect the blue and white theme and frame the floral illustration. You might consider using this project as a wall hanging. To do this, simply make the center panel, finish the edges in blue single crochet and embroider the panel from the chart. Then hang in a hallway or narrow wall area. The center panel is 18 × 48 inches and the finished afghan is approximately 40 × 51 inches.

MATERIALS

Yarn: *For afghan:* Bernat Berella "4" worsted weight acrylic (3.5 oz./100 g. skeins)—6 white, 3 blue. *For cross-stitching:* DMC Floralia 3-ply Persian yarn (the following amounts are given in yards, not skeins)—26 yds. dark green, 34 yds. light green, 10 yds. dark pink, 45 yds. light pink, 18 yds. blue, 19 yds. yellow.
Afghan hook: 14-inch I/9 (6 mm) or size needed to obtain gauge.
Crochet hook: K/10½ (7 mm)
Tapestry needle

GAUGE

4 sts = 1 inch; 4 rows = 1 inch.

Cross-stitch center panel, following the design on the chart. For cross-stitch directions see pages 26–29.

FIRST BLUE BORDER

Using the crochet hook and blue, attach yarn in upper right-hand corner.

Rnd 1: Ch 1, sc in first upright bar and each upright bar across short edge. *Ch 3 (first dc), ¼ turn (clockwise), dc into side of sc just completed and each row-end across long edge. Ch 1, ¼ turn (clockwise), 2 sc evenly spaced into side of dc just completed*, sc in each st across short end. Rep bet *s 1 time more. Join with sl st to first sc. Do not turn.

Rnd 2: Ch 1, sc in joining st and each sc across short edge. *sc in first and 3rd sts of ch-3. Ch 3 (first dc), ¼ turn (clockwise), dc into side of sc just completed and each dc across long edge, dc into side of sc. Ch 1, ¼ turn (clockwise), 2 sc evenly spaced into side of dc just completed*, sc in each sc across short edge. Rep bet *s 1 time more. Sc in remaining sts of first side worked. Join with sl st to first sc. Do not turn.

Rnds 3–4: Rep Rnd 2. Break off and fasten.

At this point, the project would look beautiful as a wall hanging and you need not continue. To complete as an afghan, you will now add a border of white.

WHITE BORDER

Using the crochet hook and white, attach yarn in first sc at upper right-hand corner.

Rnd 1: Ch 1, sc in same st, ch 3, sc in same st (corner made), [ch 3, sk next 3 sts, *sc in next st, ch 3, sk next 3 sts. Rep from * to corner; in corner work sc, ch 3, sc]. Repeat bet [ ] 2 times more. Ch 3, sk next 3 sts, **sc in next st, ch 3, sk next 3 sts. Repeat from ** across last side. Join with sl st to first sc. Do not turn.

Note: Due to variation in the number of sts, you must adjust the number of sts skipped to always have a ch-3 lp before a corner *and* to have an *odd* number of ch-3 lps across *each* side.

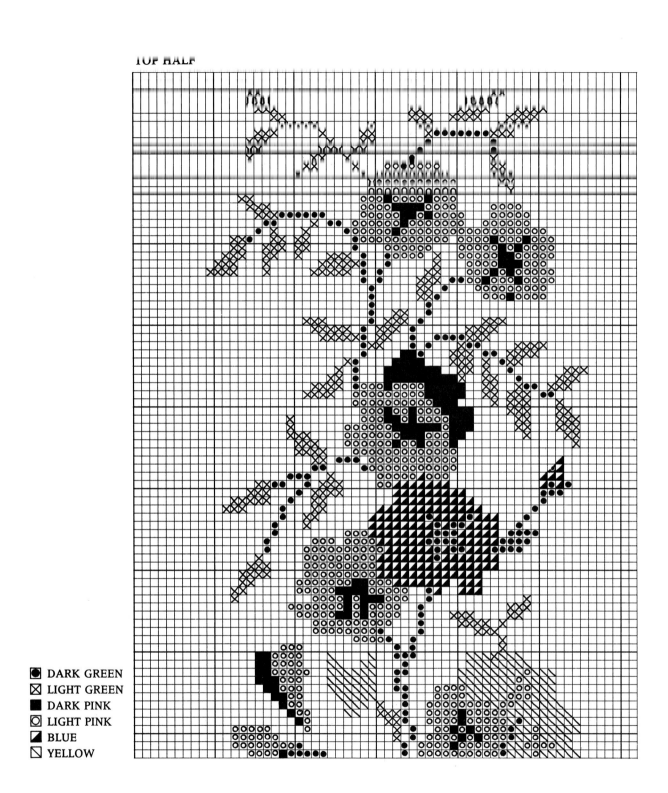

◉ DARK GREEN
⊠ LIGHT GREEN
■ DARK PINK
◎ LIGHT PINK
◪ BLUE
◹ YELLOW

Rnd 2: Sl st to ch-3 corner sp, ch 3, work 8 dc in same sp (corner made), [ch 1, sk next sc, dc in next ch-3 sp, ch 1, sk next sc, *4 dc in next ch-3 sp, ch 1, sk next sc, dc in next ch-3 sp, ch 1, sk next sc. Rep from * to corner, work 9 dc in corner ch-3 sp]. Rep bet [ ] 2 times more. Ch 1, sk next sc, dc in next ch-3 sp, ch 1, sk next sc, **4 dc in next ch-3 sp, ch 1, sk next sc, dc in next ch-3 sp, ch 1, sk next sc. Rep from ** across last side. Join with sl st to 3rd st of ch 3. Do not turn.

Rnd 3: Ch 1, sc into first ch-1 sp, [ch 3, sc bet 3rd and 4th dc of 9 corner dc, ch 3, sc bet 6th and 7th dc of 9 corner dc, *ch 3, sc in next ch-1 sp. Rep from * to corner]. Rep bet [ ] 3 times more. Join with sl st to first sc. Do not turn.

Rep Rnds 2–3 four times more, then rep Rnd 2 1 time. Break off and fasten.

SECOND BLUE BORDER

Using the crochet hook and blue, attach yarn at the 5th dc of 9 corner dc.

Rnd 1: Ch 1, sc in same st, working across short edge, sc in next 4 dc, [sk ch-1 sp, sc in next dc, sk ch-1 sp, *sc in next 4 dc, sk ch-1 sp, sc in next dc, sk ch-1 sp. Rep from * to corner, sc in first 5 dc of 9 corner dc. Ch 3 (first dc), ¼ turn (clockwise), dc into side of sc just completed, **dc in next 4 dc, sk ch-1 sp, dc in next dc, sk ch-1 sp. Rep from ** to corner; dc in first 5 dc of 9 corner dc. Ch 1, ¼ turn, 2 sc evenly spaced into dc just worked], sc in same dc of 9 corner dc as for last dc worked, sc next 4 dc. Rep bet [ ] 1 time more. Join with sl st first sc. Do not turn.

End by repeating Rnd 2 of the first blue border. Break off and fasten.

To make the afghan wider, work rows of dc back and forth across the only long edge, 8 times, or to desired width.

openwork borders that surround them. I think you'll enjoy working on this, as it is easy to carry along. It is light and airy and perfect as a light summer throw, and would make a lovely wedding gift. The finished afghan measures approximately 36 × 57 inches.

MATERIALS

Yarn: *For afghan:* Bernat Berella "4" worsted weight acrylic (3.5 oz./100 g. skeins)—6 white. *For cross-stitching:* DMC Floralia 3-ply Persian yarn (the following amounts are given in yards, not skeins)—45 yds. dark green, 20 yds. medium green, 15 yds. each of yellow and pink, 25 yds. blue, 5 yds. each of rose, lavender, and purple.

Afghan hook: 10-inch H/8 (5 mm) or size needed to obtain gauge.
Crochet hook: I/9 (6 mm)
Tapestry needle

GAUGE

7 sts = 2 inches; 4 rows = 1 inch.

CROSS-STITCH

You will note that 3 of the floral designs are repeated for the top and bottom rows of the afghan. Follow the charts to cross-stitch each rectangular motif. Make 2 each of A, B, and C. Make 1 each of D, E, and F. Count the number of squares up from the bottom of the chart and in on each side to determine where to begin the embroidery. Count the corresponding squares on your piece and start at the bottom of each flower stem, working upward across each row in 1 color, then another. For cross-stitch directions see pages 26–29.

PANEL BORDERS

The lacy stitch is worked around each afghan panel and they are then sewn or crocheted together. The lacy stitch is then worked around the assembled pieces.

Using the crochet hook, attach yarn at a corner of a panel.

Rnd 1: Ch 1, sc in same st, *ch 4, sk next 2 sts, sc in next st. Rep from * around the entire panel, being sure that lps begin and end at all corners. Join with sl st to first sc (8 lps on short edges; 16 lps on long edges). Do not turn.

Rnd 2: Ch 8 (first tr, ch 4), sc in first lp, ch 4, [*sc in next lp, ch 4. Rep from * to corner; tr in corner, ch 4]. Rep between [ ] 2 times more. **Sc in next lp, ch 4. Rep from ** across last side. Join with sl st to 4th st of ch-8. Do not turn.

Rnd 3: Rep Rnd 2. Break off and fasten.

TO FINISH

Arrange the rectangles in the following sequence: *top row:* A, B, C; *middle row:* D, E, F; *bottom row:* A, B, C. Join motifs together, either by sewing or with sc.

OUTSIDE BORDERS

Attach yarn at a corner tr. Working around the entire piece, rep Rnd 2 of the panel border 4 times, or to desired width. Break off and fasten.

CHART A

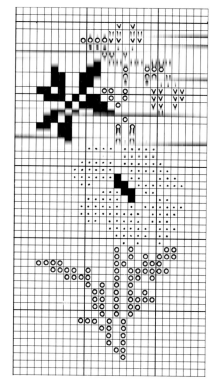

CHART B

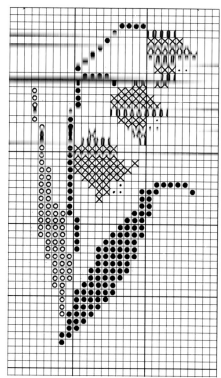

CHART C

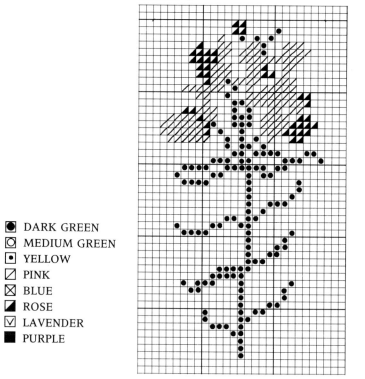

- ◕ DARK GREEN
- ◔ MEDIUM GREEN
- ⊡ YELLOW
- ◨ PINK
- ⊠ BLUE
- ◢ ROSE
- ☑ LAVENDER
- ■ PURPLE

108

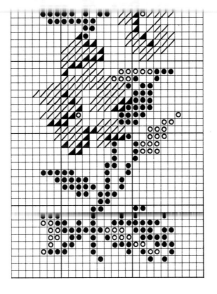

CHART E

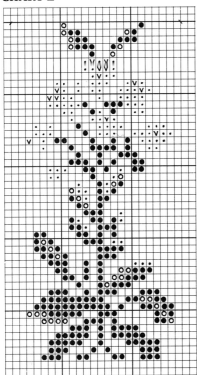

CHART F

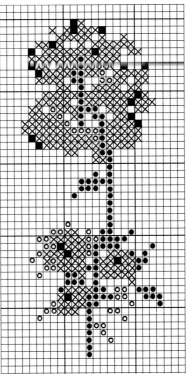

109

Hearts and Flowers

This geometric design is based on a quilt pattern with alternating checks of hearts and flowers. Made of four panels, each is covered with a background of little flower buds. The quilt squares alternate blue and pink to add interest. The hearts are burgundy red, which is repeated as edging and tassels where the panels are joined. The finished afghan is approximately 41 × 70 inches.

MATERIALS

Yarn: Bernat Berella Sportspun or any equivalent sport weight yarn (1.75 oz./50 g. balls)—22 natural (MC), 2 each of pink, dark blue, and burgundy; 1 each of green, teal blue, and pale green.
Afghan hook: 14-inch Bernat Aero F/5 (4 mm) or size needed to obtain gauge.
Crochet hook: Bernat Aero E/4 (3.5 mm)
Bernat Aero tapestry and Quickpoint needles

GAUGE

6 sts = 1 inch; 5 rows = 1 inch.

Directions

STRIP (Make 4)

Using the afghan hook and MC, ch 53. Work in the afghan st (see page 20) for 340 rows. Now, work a row of sl st as follows: Sk the first upright bar, *sl st in next upright bar. Rep from * across. Break off and fasten. Piece should measure 68 inches.

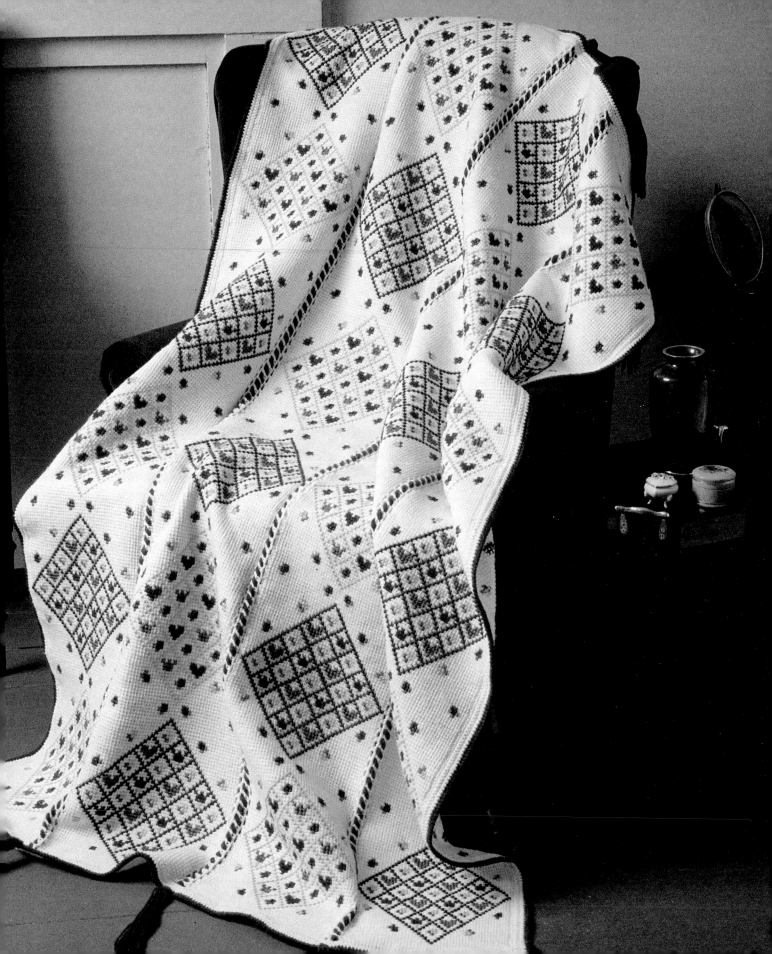

CROSS-STITCH

Starting on the 5th row from the lower edge, using tapestry needle and designated colors, follow Chart 1 and work design in cross-stitch on 2 strips. Following Chart 2, work in the same manner on the 2 remaining strips. Start at A, work to B, rep bet A and B once more, then work bet A and C. For cross-stitch directions see pages 26–29.

INNER EDGING

The inner edging forms a narrow border bet the strips. It is to be worked along the inner edges of the 4 strips. With right side facing you, start at 1 short edge and work along the long edge as follows: Using the crochet hook, join MC in the side of the first row, ch 1, 1 sc in same place as joining, *ch 3, sk next 2 rows, 1 sc in side of next row. Rep from * ending last rep 1 sc in side of last row instead of 1 sc in side of next row. Fasten off.

JOINING STRIPS

Place the strips together in the following way: *1 strip cross-stitched following Chart 1, 1 strip cross-stitched following Chart 2, rep from * once more.

With right sides facing you, using the crochet hook and MC, join yarn in the first ch sp at top of the 2nd strip, ch 1, sc in same sp, ch 1, sc in the first ch sp of the first strip; ch 1, insert hook in the next ch sp of the 2nd strip, yo hook and draw up a lp, yo and draw through both lps on hook (reverse sc); *ch 1, sc in the next ch sp of the first strip; ch 1, reverse sc in the next ch sp of the 2nd strip. Rep from * across, ending with ch 1, sl st in the last st of the 2nd strip, sl st in the last st of the first strip. Break off and fasten. Join the remaining strips in the same manner.

OUTER EDGING

Rnd 1: With right side facing you, using the crochet hook and MC, join yarn at a corner. Work a round of sc around the entire afghan, making 3 sc at each corner. Join with sl st to first sc. Do not turn.
Rnds 2–4: Ch 1, sc in each st around, making 3 sc at each corner. Join with sl st to first sc. Do not turn.
Rnd 5: With burgundy, rep Rnd 2.
Rnd 6: Working from *left to right,* work a reverse sc in each st around. Join with sl st to first reverse sc. Break off and fasten.

CHART 1

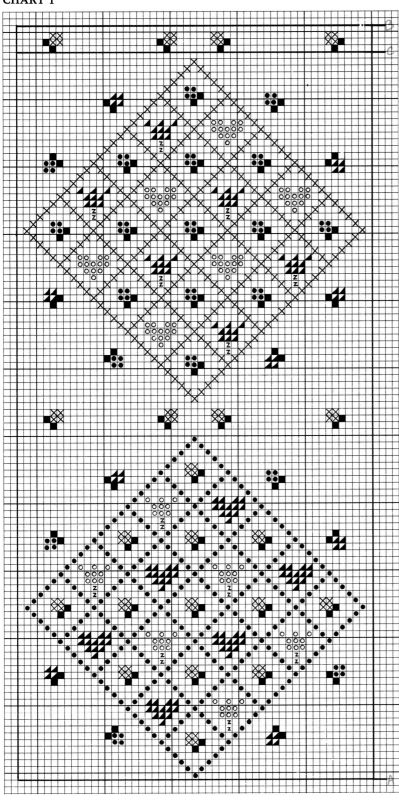

◉ PINK
⊠ DARK BLUE
◪ BURGUNDY
■ GREEN
⊡ TEAL BLUE
☑ PALE GREEN

CHART 2

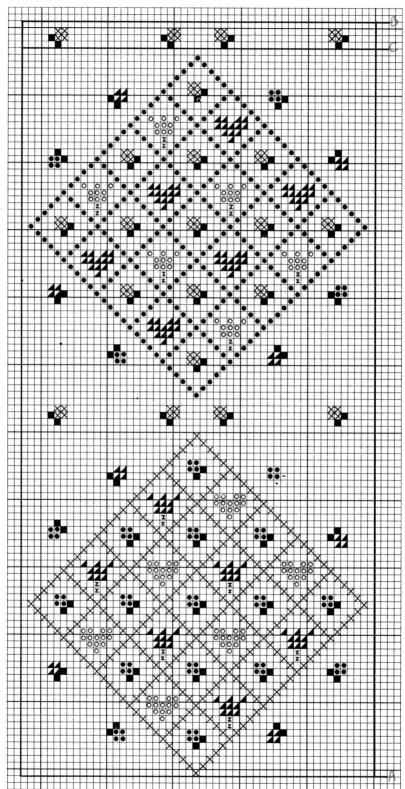

WEAVING

Cut 18 strands of burgundy yarn, 105 inches long. Thread the Quick-point needle with 6 strands. With right side of afghan facing you, starting at a short end and working into ch spaces, leave a 4-inch end, bring the needle from *back to front* of work through the first ch sp to the left of the joining row; insert the needle from *front to back* into the first ch sp to the right of the joining row, *bring the needle from *back to front* of work through the next ch sp to the left of the joining row; insert the needle from *front to back* into the next ch sp to the right of the joining row. Rep from * across, being careful not to pull the yarn too tight. Break off, leaving a 4-inch end. Secure the ends on the wrong side of the work. Weave yarn, in same manner, through the joining row of the other strips.

TO FINISH

To make the tassels, cut strands of burgundy yarn 15 inches long. Knot 10 strands at each corner and at each burgundy-colored joining on short edges. Trim ends.

Blue Mum Tapestry

Using soft pastel colors, Margaret Hendrickson designed this afghan with four wide panels joined with a line of green and a 2½-inch white border between each one. The raised green lines give the afghan an especially nice touch.

The repeat pattern reverses the position of flowers in each row to add interest. In one row the buds face to the right and in the next row they face to the left and so on. The finished afghan measures 40 × 45 inches and there is 5-inch long fringe on each end.

MATERIALS

Yarn: 4-ply worsted weight orlon or acrylic. *For afghan:* (4-oz. skeins) 8 off-white; (3.5 oz./100 g. skeins) 2 green. *For cross-stitching:* (4-oz. skeins) 1 each of medium blue, light blue, light yellow, deep yellow, bronze, and green.

Crochet hook: G/6 (4.5 mm) or size needed to obtain gauge.

Tapestry needle

GAUGE

4 sts = 1 inch; 4 rows = 1 inch.

Directions

PANEL (Make 4)

With off-white yarn, ch 27.

Row 1: Sc in 2nd ch from hook and in each ch across (26 sc).

Row 2: Ch 1, turn, sk first st, sc in next st and each st across.

Row 3: Ch 1, turn, sk first st, sc in next st and each st across, sc in turning ch. Rep Row 3 until there are 178 rows. Work a round of sc around the entire panel, making 3 sc at each corner. Join with sl st to first sc. Break off and fasten.

CROSS-STITCH

Follow the chart for placement of colors on each panel and outline stitching. The pattern is worked on 19 sts and 34 rows. Mark the center row of each panel and count 4 rows above and below to center the design vertically. Allow 8 rows between each pattern repeat. As you work each panel, alternate between working the complete chart as shown and reversing it so that adjacent flowers face in opposite directions. For cross-stitch directions, see pages 26–29.

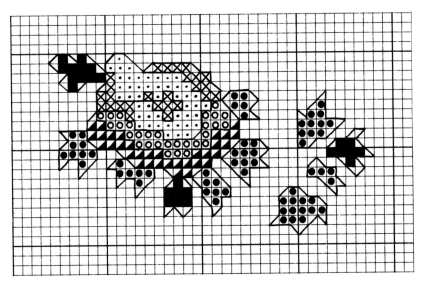

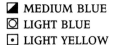 MEDIUM BLUE
◪ LIGHT BLUE
▫ LIGHT YELLOW
⊠ DEEP YELLOW
■ BRONZE
◕ GREEN
– BACKSTITCH (Use same color as the design element)

118

EDGING

With wrong side facing and using green, join yarn at corner of a panel and work a row of hdc across the long edge. Break off and fasten. Rep on the other side of the panel and on both sides of each remaining panel.

The afghan consists of 4 wide panels divided by 3 narrow off-white strips. Work the following rows on only the right-hand side of 3 strips:

With right side facing and using off-white, join yarn in hdc at the lower right-hand corner of a panel. Working across the long edge, work 3 rows of sc, 1 row of dc, and, finally, 3 rows of sc. Break off and fasten. Rep on 2 more of the panels.

JOINING

Arrange the panels as shown in the photograph. With right sides facing and using off-white, sew the panels together with overcast stitch, catching both loops of each stitch.

TO FINISH

Cut 12-inch lengths of yarn for the fringe. Use a double strand in each stitch at the short ends of the afghan. Use off-white yarn for off-white stitches and green yarn for green stitches. For fringe directions, see page 24.

Daisy Chain

Nothing says springtime like a bunch of daisies. This pretty chain of daisies decorates the center panel of the five-panel afghan. The combination of light and dark yellows adds interest when used alternately on each panel. This is a good take-along project as you can work on one strip at a time and slip it in your purse when you're on the go. The finished afghan is approximately 40 × 52 inches without the fringe.

MATERIALS

Yarn: *For afghan:* Bernat Berella "4" worsted weight yarn (3.5 oz./ 100 g. balls)—6 pale gold (A), 2 banana (B). *For cross-stitching:* DMC Floralia 3-ply Persian yarn (the following amounts are given in yards, not skeins)—30 yds. green, 34 yds. white, 5 yds. yellow.
Crochet hook: I/9 (6 mm) or size needed to obtain gauge.
Tapestry needle

GAUGE

4 sts = 1 inch; 7 rows = 2 inches.

Directions

AFGHAN STITCH PANEL

Using A, ch 40. Work the afghan st (see page 20) for 181 rows. Now, work a row of sl st as follows: Sk first upright bar, *sl st in next upright bar. Rep from * across. Break off and fasten.

The panel will be about 52 inches long. Mark the first row of the panel for the lower edge. Block the panel to 9 × 52 inches (see page 23 for blocking directions).

OPENWORK PANEL (Make 2)

Using B, ch 34 loosely.
Row 1: (right side) Sc in 2nd ch from hook, *ch 1, sk next ch, sc in next ch. Rep from * across—33 sts.
Row 2: Ch 4, turn. Sk first ch-1 sp, dc in front lp of next sc, *ch 1, sk next ch-1 sp, dc in front lp of next sc. Rep from * across—33 sts; 16 sps.
Row 3: Ch 1, turn. Sc in front lp of first dc, *ch 1, sk next ch-1 sp, sc in front lp of next dc. Rep from * across, ending with ch 1, sc in 3rd st of ch-4. Rep Rows 2 and 3 until there are 121 rows. Break off and fasten. The panel will be about 52 inches long. Mark the first row for lower edge. Block each panel to 7 × 52 inches.

CROSS-STITCH

It is easiest to do the cross-stitch on the center panel at this point, before attaching the panels. The side panels are worked on each end after the 3 center panels that you just made are joined, which makes it bulky to handle. However, if you prefer to make the entire afghan first, simply come back to the embroidery after you've made and attached all the panels.

To cross-stitch the design, count the number of squares in from each side edge of the chart and the number of squares up from the bottom edge. Then count the corresponding number of stitches on your afghan st center panel to determine where the first cross-stitch will begin. Work across with the 2 green stitches in the first row, followed by the 4 green stitches in the next row, and so on moving up the charted design. For cross-stitch directions see pages 26–29.

JOINING PANELS

With the cross-stitched panel in the center and the openwork panels on either side, sew together from the right side, using overcast st and sewing 2 rows of openwork panel to 3 rows of afghan st panel, keeping seam as elastic as crochet fabric.

SIDE PANELS (Make 2)

With the 3 center panels sewn together, the side panels are attached by working back and forth lengthwise. Using A, attach yarn to corner of an openwork panel.

Row 1: Ch 3, working across long edge, *sk sc row, work 3 dc in next sp. Rep from * across panel, ending with a dc in sc corner st.

Row 2: Ch 3, turn. Work 2 dc between first 2 dc; *work 3 dc into sp bet next two 3-dc grps. Rep from * across, ending with 3 dc bet last 2 dc.

Row 3: Ch 3, turn. *Work 3 dc into sp bet next two 3-dc grps. Rep from * across, ending with a dc in 3rd st of ch-3.

Rep Rows 2 and 3 until there are 14 rows. Break off and fasten. The panel will be 8½ inches wide.

Rep on the other side of the afghan.

TO FINISH

The fat fringes on each end of the afghan have 6 strands, and are 5 inches long and in the color of the corresponding panel. There are 15 fringes on each end of the openwork panels and 20 fringes on each end of the center panel. Cut 3 strands of yarn 10½ inches long for each fringe. For fringe directions see page 24.

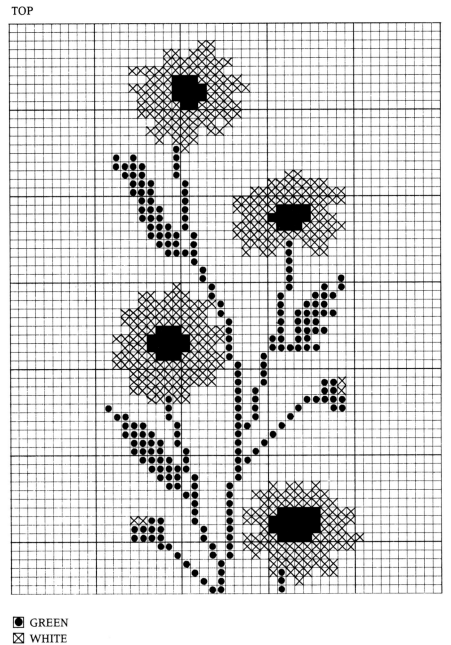

⦿ GREEN
⊠ WHITE
■ YELLOW

124

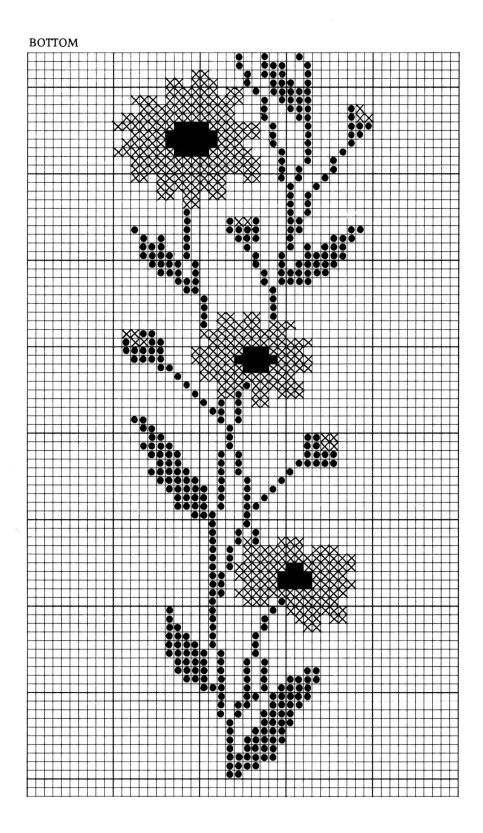

Nursery Afghans
to Treasure

*O*utfitting a nursery is an exciting part of a new baby's arrival. And the accessories are just as important as the furniture. They must be good-looking as well as useful and practical to care for. A handmade afghan can add just the right touch to the nursery and is a perfect gift for the parents-to-be. If you're awaiting a new arrival in the family, crocheting an afghan is a wonderfully relaxing way to fill leisure time and add to the joyful anticipation.

The personal aspect of an illustrated afghan makes it unique. For example, "Baby Toyland," on page 135, can be worked with an alphabet border as shown, or you can use the same charted letters to cross-stitch the afghan with your baby's name around the border. This, like all the baby afghans presented here, was made with washable yarn.

Baby Sampler

Rocking horses, blocks, hearts, sailboats, rubber duckies, these are some of the symbols that are right at home in the nursery. With its soft pastel colors, this baby sampler is a joy to make and to give. The 28 × 29–inch center panel is worked on a long afghan hook and the surrounding border is made after you've finished the embroidery. This makes it a manageable size for a carry-along cross-stitching project. The border adds 4 inches all around, making the finished size 36 × 37 inches, which is perfect for carriage or crib. The yarn is a soft and washable acrylic blend. Alternatively, you might consider making the border in one of the pastel colors rather than white, as we've done here. (See photo on overleaf.)

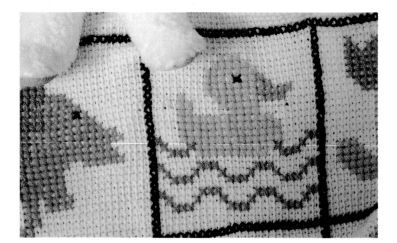

MATERIALS

Yarn: *For afghan:* Worsted weight yarn (3.5 oz./100 g. skeins)—6 white. *For cross-stitching:* Paternayan 3-ply Persian yarn (the following amounts are given in yards, not skeins)—46 yds. dark blue, 16 yds. light blue, 24 yds. yellow, 18 yds. lavender, 6 yds. pale green, 12 yds. pink, 16 yds. fuchsia.

Afghan hook: 14-inch H/8 (5 mm) or size needed to obtain gauge. (*Note:* if you use a long hook as recommended you can make the center panel in one piece)

Crochet hook: H/8 (5 mm)

Tapestry needle

GAUGE

4 sts = 1 inch; 4 rows = 1 inch.

Directions

Using the afghan hook, ch 104 (26 inches across). Work in the afghan st (see page 20) until the piece measures 27 inches long. Now, work a row of sl st as follows: Sk first upright bar, *sl st in next upright bar. Rep from * across. Break off and fasten.

CROSS-STITCH

It's important to center the design on the panel, since it will have a frame all around and you don't want more space on one side than another.

Begin by counting in 6 squares on each side edge and 5 squares up from the bottom edge of the afghan panel. Mark with a piece of colored thread. Using the dark blue yarn, follow the chart to cross-stitch the border all around.

Continue to follow the placement chart for the blue divider lines of each box that contains the design elements. Next, follow the chart to cross-stitch the nursery items. For cross-stitch directions see pages 26–29.

■ PALE GREEN
☑ LIGHT BLUE
◑ DARK BLUE
⊡ YELLOW
⊘ PINK
◪ FUCHSIA
⊠ LAVENDER

132

BORDER

Using the crochet hook, attach yarn at a corner.

Rnd 1: Ch 1, sc in first st, *ch 3, sk 2 sts, sc in next st. Rep from * around the entire piece, making sure you sc in each corner and ending with ch 3. Join with sl st to first sc. Do not turn. *Note:* you may have to make adjustments to the number of sts skipped for the corners to work out properly.

Rnd 2: Sl st in first ch-3 lp, ch 1, sc in same lp, *ch 3, sk next sc, sc in next ch-3 lp. Rep from * around, ending with ch 3. Join with sl st to first sc. Do not turn. *Note:* There will be a ch-3 lp at each corner.

Rnd 3: Sl st in first ch-3 lp, ch 1, sc in same lp, [*ch 3, sk next sc, sc in next ch-3 lp. Rep from * to corner. Ch 3, work sc, ch 3, sc in ch-3 corner lp]. Rep between [ ] 3 times more, ending with ch 3. Join with sl st to first sc. Do not turn.

Rep Rnd 3, keeping to established pattern after completing last corner of rnd, until border measures 4 inches. Break off and fasten.

TO FINISH

Tassels make a nice finishing edge for any afghan. If you'd like to finish the edges with a tassel fringe, cut 4 strands of yarn for each tassel, each 6½ inches long. For fringe directions see page 24.

Baby Toyland

This baby blanket is as soft to the touch as it looks. Wrap a newborn infant in it, use it for outings in the carriage or at home in the crib. This is the sort of afghan that is indispensable. No matter how many times you wash it, it will look brand-new. The size is ideal, the design is perfect for a baby boy or girl, and it's a project that's easy and fun to do. The alphabet chart is provided for the border design, but you might consider cross-stitching your baby's name in the center of each border to personalize this project. The finished afghan is approximately 38 × 49 inches.

MATERIALS

Yarn: Unger Fluffy worsted weight acrylic (1.75 oz./50 g. balls). *For afghan:* 11 white (MC). *For cross-stitching:* 1 each of green (A), aqua (B), blue (C), yellow (D), pink (E), fuchsia (F), and lavender (G).
Afghan hook: 14-inch I/9 (6 mm) or size needed to obtain gauge.
Crochet hook: I/9 (6 mm)
Tapestry needle

GAUGE

4 sts = 1 inch; 7 rows = 2 inches.

CHART 1

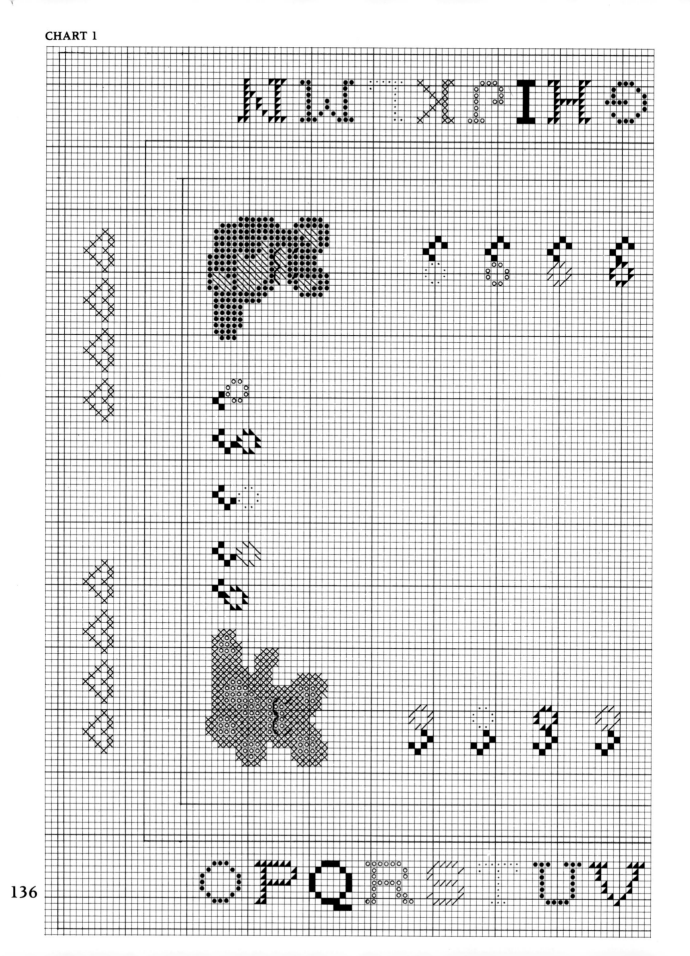

AQUA
BLUE
YELLOW
PINK
FUCHSIA
LAVENDER
GREEN
BACKSTITCH

137

Directions

CENTER PANEL

The center panel measures approximately 25 × 36 inches. Using the afghan hook and MC, ch 100. Work in the afghan st (see page 20) for 127 rows. Now, work a row of sl st as follows: Sk the first upright bar, *sl st in next upright bar. Rep from * across. Break off and fasten.

EDGING

Rnd 1: Using the crochet hook and D, sc evenly around the entire outer edge of center panel, making sure that opposite sides have the same number of sts and working 3 sc at each corner. Join with sl st to first sc. Break off and fasten D. Turn.

Rnd 2: Join MC. Working through front lps only, ch 2 (first hdc), hdc in each sc around. At all corners work 5 dc in the 2nd of the 3 corner sc. Join with sl st to 2nd ch of ch-2. Turn.

Rnd 3: Ch 2 (first hdc), working through back lps only, hdc in each hdc around. At all corners work 3 hdc in the 3rd of the 5 corner hdc. Join with sl st to 2nd ch of ch-2. Break off and fasten.

CROSS-STITCH

Note that Chart 1 and Chart 2 are the same except for the alphabet stitches in the border. Cross-stitch the design on half of the panel following Chart 1. Rep the design on the other half of the panel as shown in Chart 2. For cross-stitch directions see pages 26–29.

Using the fuchsia yarn for the blue bear and the blue yarn for the fuchsia bear, make French knots for the eyes and noses. Then, using the same color yarns, backstitch a mouth as indicated on the chart for each bear. For embroidery stitches, see page 30.

SIDE PANELS (Make 2)

The side panel measures approximately 4 × 47 inches. Using the afghan hook and MC, ch 16. Work the afghan st for 164 rows. Work a sl st row in the same manner as for center panel. Break off and fasten.

END PANELS (Make 2)

The end panel measures approximately 4 × 29 inches. Work as for side panel but for 101 rows. Work a sl st row in the same manner as for center panel. Break off and fasten. Sew the short edges of an end panel to the inside lower edges of both side panels, sewing 16 end panel sts to 14 side panel rows. This forms the border. Work other end to correspond.

INNER EDGING

Join B on wrong side. Using the crochet hook and working along the inner edge of the border, ch 2 (first hdc), hdc evenly to 1 st before corner, work a corner dec (yo hook, draw up a lp in the next st, corner st, and next st, yo and draw through all lps on hook). Work in hdc around, working a dec at the other 3 corners, making sure that opposite sides have the same number of sts. Join with sl st to 2nd ch of ch-2. Break off and fasten. Sew evenly to the center panel.

CROSS-STITCH

Follow Charts 1 and 2 for placement of stitches and cross-stitch the alphabet or, if you prefer, the baby's name. For cross-stitch directions see pages 26–29.

OUTER EDGING

Rnd 1: Join MC to a corner. With right side facing and crochet hook, ch 3 (first dc), [*sk next st, dc in next st, dc in skipped st (cross st). Rep from * to next corner, 5 dc in corner]. Rep between [ ] 3 times more. Join with sl st to 3rd ch of ch-3.

Rnd 2: Ch 1, *sc in first dc, ch 2, sc in the 2nd ch from the hook (picot), sk next dc. Rep from * around. Join with sl st to first sc. Break off and fasten.

Sweet Baby Buds

A cluster of delicate yellow and white flowers growing on a field of lavender is a sweet design for a baby blanket. The openwork border and picot edging add interest to the center panel and frame the cross-stitch illustration. The finished afghan is approximately 27 × 34 inches, which is just right for a newborn infant or for use as a lap throw. Because of its small size, you can easily make the afghan in a couple of days. The cross-stitching will work up quickly as well.

MATERIALS

Yarn: *For afghan:* Bernat Berella "4" worsted weight acrylic (3.5 oz./100 g. skeins)—4 lavender, 1 white. *For cross-stitching:* DMC Floralia 3-ply Persian yarn (the following amounts are given in yards, not skeins)—18 yds. white, 3 yds. purple, 28 yds. yellow, and 35 yds. green.
Afghan hook: I/9 (6 mm) or size needed to obtain gauge.
Crochet hook: H/8 (5 mm)
Tapestry needle

GAUGE

5 sts = 1 inch; 4 rows = 1 inch.

Directions

Using the afghan hook and lavender, ch 87. Work in the afghan st (see page 20) for 95 rows. Now, work a row of sl st as follows: Sk the first upright bar, *sl st in next upright bar. Rep from * across. Do not break off. Transfer the remaining lp from the afghan hook to the crochet hook to work the edging.

EDGING

Rnd 1: Ch 1, *sc, ch 1, sc in corner; 97 sc across long edge to corner; sc, ch 1, sc in corner; 93 sc across short edge to corner. Rep from * 1 time more. Join with sl st to first sc. Do not turn.

Rnd 2: Ch 3 (first dc); (dc, ch 1, dc) in ch-1 sp (corner made); *dc in next sc, ch 1, sk next sc, (dc in next 3 sc, ch 1, sk next sc) 24 times, dc in next sc; dc, ch 1, dc in ch-1 sp (corner made); dc in next sc, ch 1, sk next sc, (dc in next 3 sc, ch 1, sk next sc) 23 times*, dc in next sc; work corner as before. Rep bet *s 1 time more. Join with sl st to 3rd st of ch-3. Do not turn.

Rnd 3: Ch 1, sc in same st as joining, sc in each dc and in each ch around, working 3 sc in each ch-1 corner sp. Join with sl st to first sc. Do not turn.

Rnd 4: Ch 3 (first dc), dc in next 2 sc; ch 3, sk 2nd of 3 corner sc (corner made); *(dc in next 3 sc, ch 1, sk next sc) 25 times, dc in next 3 sc; ch 3, sk 2nd of 3 corner sc (corner made); (dc in next 3 sc, ch 1, sk next sc) 24 times*, dc in next 3 sc; ch 3, sk 2nd of 3 corner sc (corner made). Rep bet *s 1 time more. Join with sl st to 3rd st of ch-3. Do not turn.

Rnd 5: Ch 1, sc in each dc and in each ch around, working 5 sc in each ch-3 corner sp. Join with sl st to first sc. Do not turn.

Rnd 6: Ch 3 (first dc), dc in next 2 sc, ch 1, sk next sc; *dc in next sc; dc, ch 3, dc in next sc (corner made); dc in next sc, ch 1, sk next sc, (dc in next 3 sc, ch 1, sk next sc) 26 times, dc in next sc; dc, ch 3, dc in next sc (corner made); dc in next sc, ch 1, sk next sc *, (dc in next 3 sc, ch 1, sk next sc) 25 times. Rep bet *s 1 time more, then (dc in next 3 sc, ch 1, sk next sc) 24 times. Join with sl st to the 3rd st of ch-3. Do not turn.

Rnd 7: Rep Rnd 5.

Rnd 8: Ch 3, dc in each sc around, working 3 dc in 3rd of 5 corner sc. Join with sl st to 3rd st of ch-3. Do not turn.

Rnd 9: Ch 1, sc in each dc around, working 3 sc in 2nd of 3 corner dc. Join with sl st to first sc. Break off and fasten.

PICOT EDGING

With right side facing, and using crochet hook, join white with a sl st in the 2nd of any 3 corner sc. *Ch 3, sl st in 3rd ch from hook (picot made), sc in same st; sc in next 6 sts. Rep from * around entire piece, adjusting the number of sc between picots to have a picot at each corner. Join with sl st to first sc. Break off and fasten.

CROSS-STITCH

Follow the chart to cross-stitch each color as indicated. For this design you might find it best to fill in all the green areas for the stems and leaves first, then stitch each of the flowers, and finish 1 color before working with another. The center of each flower should be done last. For cross-stitch direction see pages 26–29.

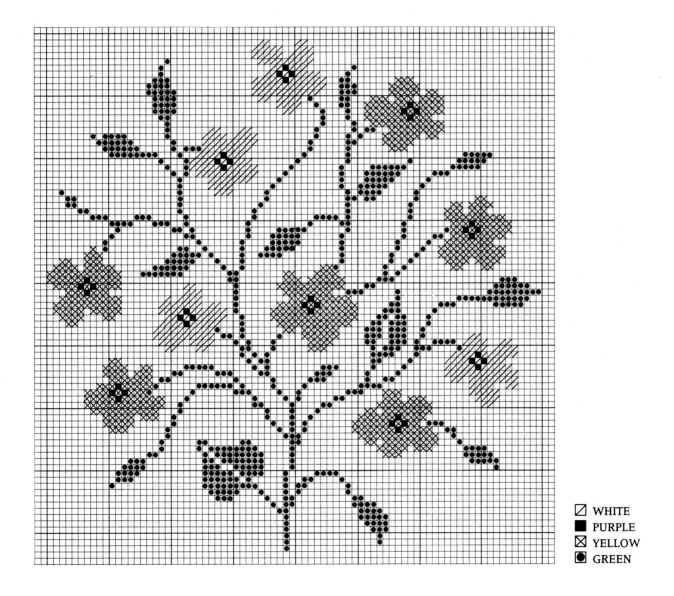

☑ WHITE
■ PURPLE
⊠ YELLOW
◉ GREEN

143

Bundled Babies

This whimsical afghan was designed and made by Mary Smith, who has been creating adorable crocheted projects all her life. Each row contains five babies bundled in a pink or blue bunting. And, like real babies, each is unique. There are brown, black, and white babies; some with braided hair, some with tousled red, brown, or blond hair. All are sleeping peacefully with smiles on their faces. The finished afghan is 27 × 55 inches, which is a good crib-size blanket.

MATERIALS

Yarn: *For afghan:* 4-ply acrylic yarn—10 oz. each of blue (A) and pink (B), 12 oz. of white, 2 oz. each of tan (C) and light pink (D), scraps of different colors for hair. *For embroidery:* 3-ply yarn—small amounts of red, blue, pink, and white.
Crochet hook: G/6 (4.5 mm) or size needed to obtain gauge.
Tapestry needle

GAUGE

5 sc = 1 inch; 4 rows = 1 inch.

Directions

MOTIF (Make 25: 12 of one color; 13 of the other)

Note: Ch 1 to turn each row. To change colors, work last lp of old color off with the new color.

Begin with A or B and ch 18.
Row 1: Sc in the 2nd ch from hook, hdc in next ch, (sc in next ch, hdc in next ch) 7 times, sc in last ch.
Row 2: (Hdc in next st, sc in next st) 8 times, hdc in last st.
Row 3: (Sc in next st, hdc in next st) 8 times, sc in last st.
Rows 4–17: Rep Rows 2 and 3.
Row 18: Working in back lps only, rep Row 2.

Row 19: Rep Row 3.

Row 20: (Hdc in next st, sc in next st) 3 times, drop yarn; attach C or D, sc in next 5 sts, drop yarn; attach a 2nd ball of A or B, (sc in next st, hdc in next st) 3 times.

Row 21: (Sc in next st, hdc in next st) 2 times, sc in next st, drop yarn; pick up C or D, sc in next 7 sts, drop yarn; pick up A or B, (sc in next st, hdc in next st) 2 times, sc in last st.

Row 22: (Hdc in next st, sc in next st) 2 times, drop yarn; pick up C or D, sc in next 9 sts, drop yarn; pick up A or B, (sc in next st, hdc in next st) 2 times.

Row 23: Sc in next st, hdc in next st, sc in next st, drop yarn; pick up C or D, sc in next 11 sts, drop yarn; pick up A or B, sc in next st, hdc in next st, sc in last st.

Row 24: Hdc in next st, sc in next st, hdc in next st, drop yarn; pick up C or D, sc in next 11 sts, drop yarn; pick up A or B, hdc in next st, sc in next st, hdc in last st.

Row 25: Rep Row 23.

Row 26: Rep Row 22.

Row 27: Attach white, sc in next st, drop yarn; pick up A or B, (hdc in next st, sc in next st) 2 times, drop yarn; pick up C or D, sc in next 7 sts, cut yarn; pick up A or B, (sc in next st, hdc in next st) 2 times, drop yarn; attach 2nd ball of white and sc in last st.

Row 28: Sc in next 2 sts, drop yarn; pick up A or B, (hdc in next st, sc in next st) 6 times, hdc in next st, drop yarn; pick up white, sc in last 2 sts.

Row 29: Sc in next 3 sts, drop yarn; pick up A or B, (hdc in next st, sc in next st) 5 times, hdc in next st, drop yarn; pick up white, sc in last 3 sts.

Row 30: Sc in next 4 sts, drop yarn; pick up A or B, (hdc in next st, sc in next st) 4 times, hdc in next st, drop yarn; pick up white, sc in last 4 sts.

Row 31: Sc in next 5 sts, cut yarn; pick up A or B, (hdc in next st, sc in next st) 3 times, hdc in next st, cut yarn; pick up white, sc in last 5 sts.

Rows 32–36: Sc in each st. Do not break off.

EDGING

Rnd 1: Sc evenly around entire outer edge, working 3 sc at each corner. Join with sl st to first sc. Do not turn.

Rnd 2: Ch 2 (first hdc), hdc in each st around, working 3 hdc in 2nd of 3 corner sc. Join with sl st to 2nd st of ch-2. Break off and fasten.

BUNTING TURN-BACK

Join A or B in the skipped front lp of Row 18.

Row 1: Sc in first st, (sc in next st, hdc in next st) 6 times.

Row 2: Sc first 2 sts tog, (sc in next st, hdc in next st) 5 times, sc in last st.

Row 3: Sc in the first st, catching first st of Row 21, (sc in next st, hdc in next st) 3 times, sc next 2 sts tog, sl st in last 3 sts. Break off and fasten.

Weave in all loose ends.

Optional: For a decorative touch, Mary added 3 cross-stitches to the blanket turn-back.

EMBROIDERY

Faces (see drawing): Separate the strands of yarn and rejoin 2 strands to embroider the facial features with a backstitch (page 28). Use blue yarn for the eyes and red yarn for the mouths.

Hair: Cut and loop short strands of yarn at the top of heads for hair. Trim to desired length or make braids and tie ends with bows made from the pink or blue yarn.

JOINING MOTIFS

Arrange the motifs so you have 5 rows of 5 different motifs across and down. You can alternate blue and pink, or arrange the sections as Mary did or in a way that you think looks best. Then, with wrong sides facing, using crochet hook and white, join the sections tog with sl st.

TO FINISH

With right side facing, and using crochet hook, join MC in a corner and work 1 rnd of reverse sc around the afghan as follows: *Swing hook downward across the material from *left to right* and insert into next st to the *right*, yo and draw a lp through, yo and draw through both lps on hook. Rep from * around, taking care to keep work flat. Join with sl st to first reverse sc. Break off and fasten.

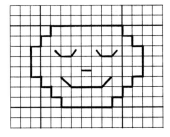

BACKSTITCH FOR FACES

"Shhh, Baby's Sleeping!"

This adorable afghan with a curled-up sleeping bear is just perfect for any new baby. Use it in the crib or carriage for your own baby or grandchild, or make it to give as a very special gift. The pretty lacy border adds just the right delicate touch around the center panel.

This project is made with Bernat Sportspun and is completely washable. The finished afghan is 37 × 53 inches. And would you believe, the baby kittens in the basket were born just minutes before this photograph was taken!

MATERIALS

Yarn: *For afghan:* Bernat Berella Sportspun or any equivalent sport weight yarn (1.75 oz./50 g. skeins)—13 white. *For cross-stitching:* DMC Floralia 3-ply Persian yarn (the following amounts are given in yards, not skeins)—27 yds. medium pink, 11 yds. each of aqua and light yellow, 38 yds. medium brown, 5½ yds. each of peach, beige, and dark brown; DMC embroidery yarn (8.7 yd. skein)—1 tan, 2 very dark brown.
Afghan hook: 14-inch Bernat Aero H/8 (5 mm) or size needed to obtain gauge.
Crochet hook: Bernat Aero H/8 (5 mm)
Bernat Aero tapestry needle

GAUGE

9 sts = 2 inches; 4 rows = 1 inch.

■ MEDIUM PINK
◑ AQUA
▨ LIGHT YELLOW
⊠ MEDIUM BROWN
⊡ PEACH
⊡ BEIGE
■ DARK BROWN
─ BACKSTITCH (Outline yellow with tan; outline brown with dark brown)

150

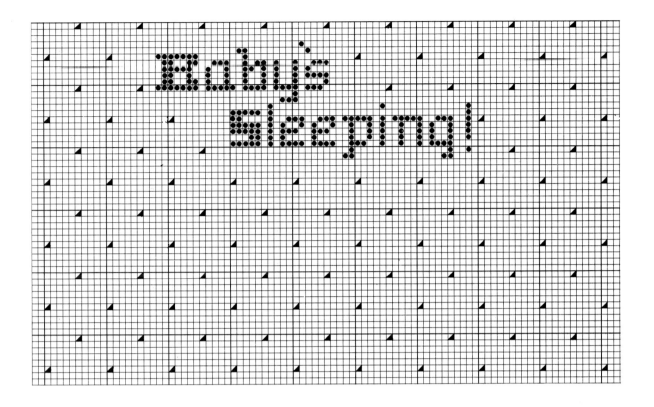

Directions

CENTER PANEL

Using the afghan hook, ch 145. Work in the afghan st (see page 20) for 192 rows. Now, work a row of sl st as follows: Sk first upright bar, *sl st in next upright bar. Rep from * across. The piece should measure 48 inches. Do not break off.

EDGING

Rnd 1: Insert crochet hook in remaining lp, ch 1, work *191 sc across long edge to corner, 3 sc in corner, 143 sc across short edge to corner, 3 sc in corner. Rep from * 1 time more. Join with sl st to first sc. Do not turn.

Rnd 2: Ch 3 (first hdc, ch 1), sk next sc, [*hdc in next sc, ch 1, sk next sc. Rep from * to corner. Work hdc, ch 1, hdc in 2nd of 3 corner sc, ch 1, sk next sc]. Rep between [ ] 3 times more. Join with sl st to 2nd st of ch-3. Do not turn.

Rnd 3: Sl st in first ch-1 sp, ch 4 (first dc, ch 1), sk next hdc, [*dc in next ch-1 sp, ch 1, sk next hdc. Rep from * to corner. Work dc, ch 1, dc in ch-1 corner sp, ch 1, sk next hdc]. Rep between [ ] 3 times more; ending with dc in last ch-1 sp, ch 1. Join with sl st to 3rd st of ch-3. Do not turn.

Rnd 4: Sl st across next ch-1 sp, next dc, next ch-1 sp, and into next dc; ch 3 (first dc), sk next ch-1 sp and next dc, *in next ch-1 sp (yo, insert hook in sp, yo, draw up a lp, yo, draw through 2 lps, yo, draw through 1 lp) 2 times, yo, draw through all lps on hook (cluster made), ch 4. Work another cluster in the same ch-1 sp, sk next dc and next ch-1 sp, dc in next dc, sk next ch-1 sp and next dc. Rep from * around; end by working cluster, ch 4, cluster in the next-to-last ch-1 sp, sk last dc and last ch-1 sp. Join with sl st to 3rd st of ch-3. Do not turn. *Note:* There will be a cluster grp at each corner ch-1 sp.

Rnd 5: Ch 1, sc in first dc, ch 3, *sk next cluster; in next ch-4 sp work sc, ch 3, sc; sk next cluster, ch 3, sc in next dc, ch 3. Rep from * around; ending with sk next cluster; in last ch-4 sp work sc, ch 3, sc, ch 3, sk last cluster. Join with sl st to first sc. Do not turn.

Rnd 6: Ch 1, sc in first ch-3 sp, *ch 1, sk next sc; in next ch-3 sp work (cluster, ch 3) 2 times, cluster; (ch 1, sk next sc, sc in next ch-3 sp) 2 times. Rep from * around; ending with ch 1, sk next sc; in next-to-last ch-3 sp work (cluster, ch 3) 2 times, cluster; ch 1, sk last sc, sc in last ch-3 sp, ch 1. Join with sl st to first sc.

Rnd 7: Ch 1, sl st in first sc, *ch 3, sk next ch-1 sp, (sk next cluster; in next ch-3 sp work sc, ch 3, sc, ch 3) 2 times, sk next cluster, sk next ch-1 sp, sc in next sc, sk next ch-1 sp, sc in next sc. Rep from * around. Join with sl st to first st of ch-3. Break off and fasten.

CROSS-STITCH

Following the chart, count upright bars, leaving 23 rows free on the lower and upper edges and 27 sts free on each side. Using 2 strands of Floralia, cross-stitch, following the chart. For cross-stitch directions see pages 26–29.

TO FINISH

Using the embroidery yarn as it comes from the skein and following the chart, backstitch (see page 28) the outline of the sleeping bear.

Tumbling Clowns

Each square of this playful afghan is worked individually and then stitched together in three rows of three each. The position of each square creates an afghan of tumbling clowns. Worked in primary colors, this afghan will delight any child or parent. Five of the clowns wear red suits and blue hats and four wear blue suits with red hats. Each square is done with the afghan stitch and measures 10 × 10 inches.

This is a perfect carry-along project. The squares are small enough to fit in a purse, and once the background is finished, it's easy to take embroidery yarn and needle along with the chart for cross-stitching.

After completing the first square, I found it easier to use this as a guide rather than referring to the chart when making the other squares. Remember to change color placement for the appropriate number of blue and red clowns. The finished afghan measures approximately 33 × 33 inches.

Note: This afghan can be made in three strips, each 10 × 30 inches, rather than individual and joined squares. In this case, you'll be working on three clown designs at a time and joining the three long panels when finished. It will still be a portable project, but not as compact. If you do it this way, be sure to alternate red and blue clowns and position them according to the assembly diagram. Doing it this way is not as foolproof as working on the individual squares, but it's an option.

MATERIALS

Yarn: *For afghan:* Bernat Berella "4" worsted weight acrylic (3.5 oz./100 g. skeins)—6 white. *For cross-stitching:* DMC Floralia 3-ply Persian yarn (the following amounts are given in yards, not skeins)—45 yds. blue, 22 yds. yellow, 55 yds. each of red and pink, 18 yds. orange, 40 yds. green, 2 yds. black.
Afghan hook: 14-inch I/9 (6 mm) or size needed to obtain gauge.
Crochet hook: G/6 (4.5 mm)
Tapestry needle

GAUGE

5 sts = 1 inch; 9 rows = 2 inches.

Directions

SQUARE (Make 9 squares, 10 × 10 inches)

Using the afghan hook, ch 51. Work in the afghan st (see page 20) until the piece measures 10 inches. Now, work a row of sl st as follows: Sk first upright bar, *sl st in next upright bar. Rep from * across. Break off and fasten.

CROSS-STITCH

Follow the chart for placement of cross-stitches. Beginning with the green embroidery yarn, the first stitch is placed 20 stitches in from the right-hand edge and 7 rows up from the bottom of each square. Follow the chart for placement of each color. Don't forget that 5 clowns have red suits with blue hats and that 4 reverse these colors. For cross-stitch directions see pages 26–29.

JOINING SQUARES

Refer to the diagram for arranging the rows of clowns. Beginning with a red (A) clown, alternate blue (B) clowns and red clowns in each row as shown. Note that the clowns are positioned so that they appear to be tumbling over the afghan. Sew squares together.

EDGING

Rnd 1: Using the crochet hook, attach yarn in a corner and sc evenly around the entire piece, working 3 sc at each corner. Join with sl st to first sc. Do not turn.
Rnd 2: Ch 1, *sc in next 3 sts, ch 3, sc in last sc (picot made). Rep from * around. Join with sl st to first sc. Break off and fasten.

CLOWN A

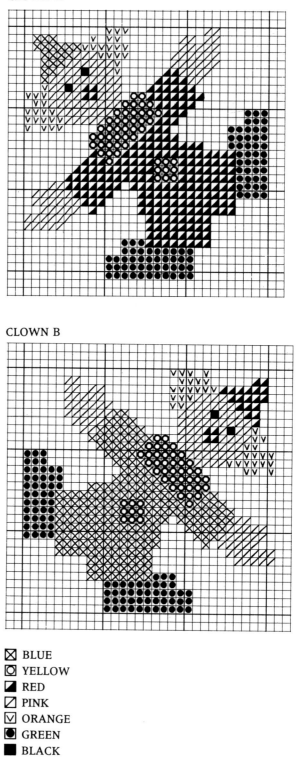

CLOWN B

⊠ BLUE
⊙ YELLOW
◪ RED
◹ PINK
▽ ORANGE
◉ GREEN
■ BLACK

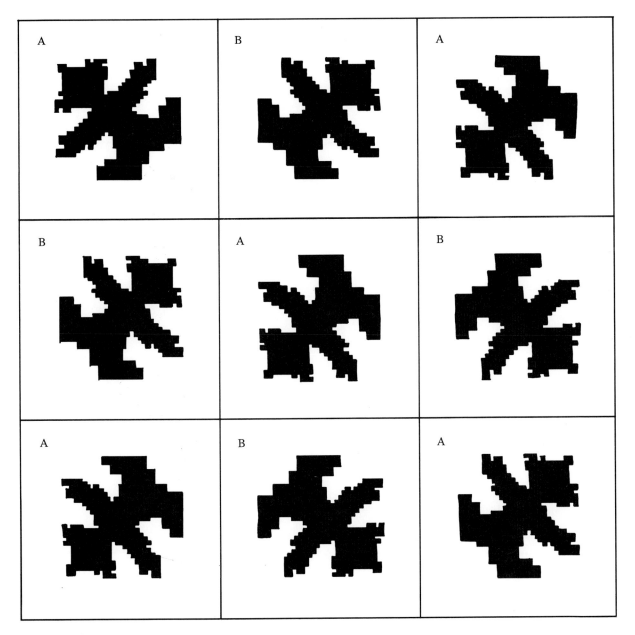

A = RED
B = BLUE

157

This Little Piggy

"This little piggy went to market, this little piggy stayed home . . ." is a refrain familiar to every baby. And what a delightful theme to embroider on an afghan! The white bands across the top and bottom are each decorated with three fat, pink pigs. The center panel is worked in the afghan stitch so you can embroider the first line of the popular verse in the middle of the afghan. We chose yellow for the divider bands, but you can choose any color. It might be blue or pale green or even pink, to match the piglets. The finished size is approximately 25 × 34 inches.

MATERIALS

Yarn: *For afghan:* Bernat Berella "4" worsted weight yarn (3.50 oz./ 100 g. skeins)—3 white (MC), 3 yellow (CC). *For cross-stitching:* DMC Floralia 3-ply Persian yarn (following amounts are given in yards, not skeins)—90 yds. pink, 36 yds. lavender, small amount black.
Afghan hook: 14-inch G/6 (4.5 mm) or size needed to obtain gauge.
Tapestry needle

GAUGE

5 sts = 1 inch; 9 rows = 2 inches.

Directions

For consistency in tension and gauge, the entire afghan was worked on the afghan hook even though only the cross-stitched areas are worked in the afghan st. The narrow yellow bands and wide yellow center panel are done in sc, worked into lps of sts in the previous row.

Using the afghan hook and yellow, ch 122.
Row 1: Sc in 2nd ch from hook and in each ch across—121 sc.
Row 2: Ch 1, turn, sk first st, sc in next st and in each st across.
Row 3: Ch 1, turn, sk first st, sc in next st and in each st across, sc in turning ch.

Rep Row 3 until there are 8 rows. With white, work in the afghan st (see page 20) for 32 rows. With yellow, rep Row 3 eighty times. With white, work in the afghan st for 32 rows. With yellow, rep Row 3 eight times more. Break off and fasten.

CROSS-STITCH

It's important that the piglets be centered and evenly spaced on the bands of white at the top and bottom of the afghan. Before starting, refer to the chart and count the exact number of unworked squares on the chart from each side edge to where the first pink stitch is to be placed. Count the corresponding number of squares in from each side of the afghan to determine where to place the first stitch for the pigs at each end.

Next, be sure there are exactly the same number of unworked stitches on both sides of the center pig so that all 3 pigs are evenly spaced. Do the same on the top and bottom of each pig so they are equally centered on the bands.

Piglets' eyes are black; tails are backstitched in pink (see page 28).

Use lavender and follow the chart to cross-stitch the verse in the center of the yellow panel. Take the same care as for the placement of the pigs, to be sure the verse is centered and that the letters are evenly spaced as shown. For cross-stitch directions see pages 26–29.

TO FINISH

If you'd like to finish this afghan with a fringe of white and yellow tassels at each end, cut 6½-inch lengths in both colors for each tassel. For fringe directions see page 24.

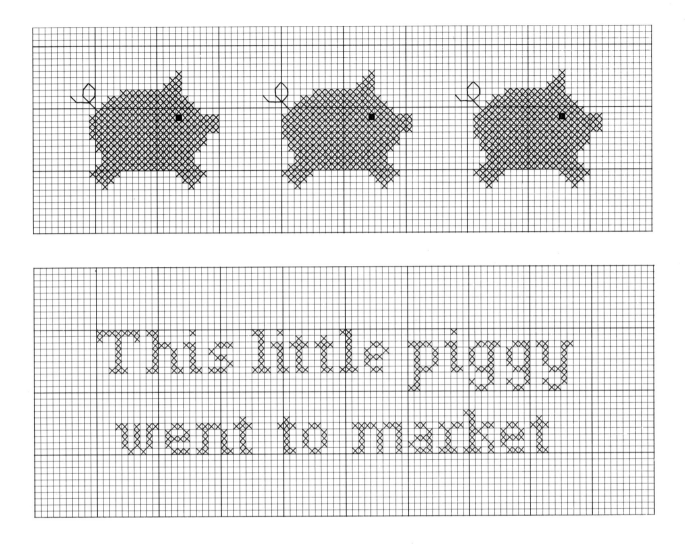

CROSS-STITCH PIGS IN PINK
CROSS-STITCH EYES IN BLACK
CROSS-STITCH LETTERS IN LAVENDER
BACKSTITCH TAILS IN PINK

Child's Art in Stitches

If you have leftover yarn and want to use it in an interesting way, consider this idea that comes from Joan Roche. It's so cute that I thought it worth passing along as something you might like to create for yourself. Joan suggested that her four-year-old grandchild, Sarah Stevens, send her grandmother a package of her artwork. It contained her first letters, a picture of a pig, stick figures for her family (minus the arms for one member), and her house. Grandma Joan then reproduced the art, without adding the missing arms, in cross-stitch on an afghan for Sarah. She used the leftover yarn from her projects on pages 51 and 73.

Using graph paper with four squares to the inch, Joan charted each of the pictures and then added Sarah's name and age at the top. You can use the cross-stitch alphabet letters on page 165 for this part of the project, but since each child's drawing is unique, you'll have to chart your own picture. It's easy to do, since children's drawings are fairly simple. See the photograph of Sarah's artwork and the charts for reference. The finished afghan, without the 2-inch fringe at each end, is 27 × 30 inches.

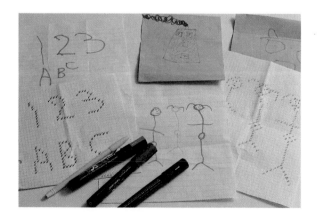

MATERIALS

Yarn: *For afghan:* Bernat Sesame worsted weight wool or Berella "4" worsted weight acrylic (3.5 ozs./100 g. skeins)—3 natural. *For cross-stitching:* Leftover scraps of different colors.
Afghan hook: 14-inch H/8 (5 mm) or size needed to obtain gauge.
Tapestry needle

GAUGE

7 sts = 2 inches; 3 rows = 1 inch.

Directions

Ch 95. Work in the afghan st (see page 20) until the piece measures 30 inches long, or to desired length.

CROSS-STITCH

When the background is finished you will want to plan your design and where each element will be placed. A rule of thumb for figuring out how much yarn you will need for each color is 23 cross-stitches to the yard. For cross-stitch directions see pages 26–29.

TO FINISH

Cut 4-inch lengths of yarn for the fringe. For fringe directions see page 24.

164

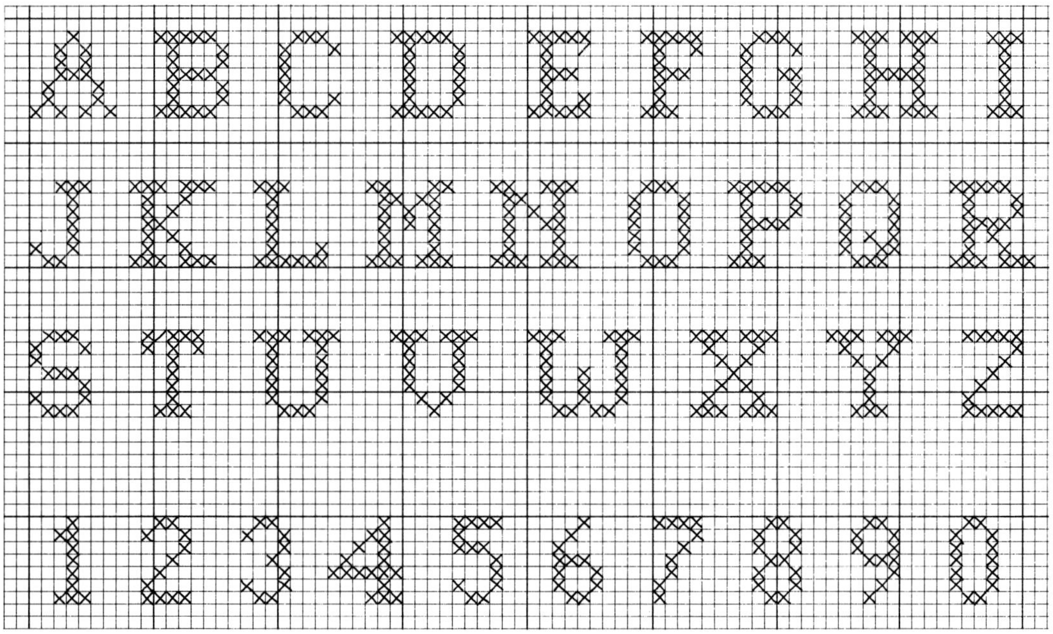

Index

All of us at Sedgewood® Press are dedicated to offering you, our customer, the best books we can create. We are particularly concerned that all of the instructions for making the projects are clear and accurate. We welcome your comments and would like to hear any suggestions you may have. Please address your correspondence to Customer Service Department, Sedgewood® Press, Meredith Corporation, 750 Third Avenue, New York, NY 10017.

For information on how you can have *Better Homes and Gardens* delivered to your door, write to: Robert Austin, P.O. Box 4536, Des Moines, IA 50336.

Printed in the United States of America